C. GRATTON KEMP is Professor of Education at The Ohio State University. He holds a B.A. from the University of Toronto; B.D. from Union Theological Seminary; M.A. and Ed.D. from Columbia; and Ph.D. from Michigan State University. He has been both a teacher and counselor for many years, and along with his work at Ohio State, Professor Kemp participates in church workshops, leadership training camps, and similar groups using the group process. He has taught summer sessions at the University of Hawaii and McGill University, as well as others. Previous books by this author include *Perspectives on the Group Process, Intangibles in Counseling,* and *Foundations of Group Counseling.*

SMALL GROUPS AND SELF-RENEWAL

By the author:

FOUNDATIONS OF GROUP COUNSELING

INTANGIBLES IN COUNSELING

PERSPECTIVES ON THE GROUP PROCESS

Small Groups and Self-Renewal

C. GRATTON KEMP

THE SEABURY PRESS
NEW YORK

Library of Congress Catalog Card Number: 72-147949
Design by Carol Basen
709-371-C-3.5
Printed in the United States of America

To Arline and Elizabeth

PREFACE

The story of man is the story of small groups. Man renews himself in his relationship with others. Today persons in all walks of life deeply sense the need for meaningful interaction. Many look to the small group to supply this. But there is no mystique in the small group. Nothing magical should be expected to take place when people sit in a circle and interact. Personal renewal can result only to the degree that certain conditions exist. This book is concerned with those conditions.

Many books have been written on the group process for the sophisticated professional. Few, if any, have been written for the unsophisticated majority who would like to know about groups, become members of groups or learn to be group leaders. This book should be helpful to both the sophisticated professional and those who are not. Its logical format and clear descriptions should make it especially useful to those who are inexperienced in this line of endeavor.

This book has three emphases: the exploration and clarification of (1) the foundation of the group in several disciplines and in the changing concepts of civilization; (2) the nature of various groups—theories, methods, problems, needed skills, and evaluation processes; and (3) leadership preparation and application of group process to the various aspects of life and work.

The following premises provide a consistent basis for understanding the content: (1) The possibilities of group process for self-renewal are based on the potentialities and limitations of man himself. (2) The realization of these possibilities is directly related to man's openness to experience, knowledge, skills, and interest in becoming. (3) The concept of individual differences is basic to the provision of the optimal helping relationship. (4) Ability to participate and benefit from the group experience is a developmental process. (5) Group process enhances the potential for change in the perceptions and self-concepts of the members.

The book is planned for both lay and professional workers in the church, in the school, and in social, business, and recreational organizations who are involved in the constructive development of persons through the group experience. It is hoped that members and leaders in these organizations will find the discussion of the various aspects of group process useful in the gaining of ideas and in the improvement of their functioning.

Many persons contributed directly and indirectly to the writing of this book. Children, youth, and adults in various churches, schools, hospitals, and recreational settings both here and abroad have participated with me in small groups, sharing their ideas and insights. College students participating in the analysis of the group climate and process have advanced my understanding. Associations with colleagues in college and church and the support of friends have helped to make the writing possible. I am also indebted to those who have contributed directly, especially to the democratic, flexible, judicious, and wise suggestions of the editor, Arthur R. Buckley, and to my wife, Arline, to whom the book is dedicated, for her encouragement, suggestions, and critical reading of the manuscript, and also to our daughter, Elizabeth, whose disturbing questions are so frequently a needed challenge.

C. Gratton Kemp

The Ohio State University
Columbus, Ohio

CONTENTS

SMALL GROUPS
AND
SELF-RENEWAL

1 GROUP ISSUES AND POSSIBILITIES TODAY

The Small Group—Past and Present

Man has always lived in groups. Such designations as *family, clan, tribe* and *gang* have a long history. New lands have been discovered, new governments established, new industries organized. New social organizations, religious beliefs, denominations and churches have all emerged through the efforts of groups.

In relation to current needs, groups of many kinds have grown up spontaneously. They have been and still are the products of their environments. Their nature is a function of the times and a reflection of understandings from many areas of thought and study. Every branch of organized knowledge influences and molds the nature and functioning of groups to some degree.

Among these molding influences are the evolving concepts regarding man—what is significant about him, the society he builds, and his own development. Groups play a part in all of these aspects. The organization of groups and how they function reflect the current knowledge and understanding of man himself.

GROUPS IN THE 1890'S

Groups in the latter part of the nineteenth century resembled groups today only distantly. They differed because the times differed. Man was considered significant chiefly because of his capacity for thought and rational decision-making. His emotions were unimportant and what conscience might have told him was frequently neglected. In other words he used his powers of reasoning to make decisions, and he used his will to carry them out. If his emotions got in his way, they were repressed. The structure of society, home, school, office, business, and industry was authoritarian. The leader was the one who knew and who could get things done. The majority did his bidding. They worked for him, voted for him and respected him, not always for his personhood but because of what he could do. The leader provided rewards for this allegiance, generally monetary and status, but he also assumed responsibility for the results.

Compartmentalization was the order of the day. The home was one world, work a different one, the social yet another. A strict separation was maintained among the different aspects of life including that between the secular and the religious. Religion reflected the authoritarian posture of the culture. Rewards and punishments were emphasized. Guilt and grace were at the center of life and received attention as matters of deep concern.

Learning through association was the general practice. It was assumed that there were fixed bodies of knowledge which were relevant and needed in order to be informed. The educator in the various fields determined what should be learned, in what order and in what planned degree of difficulty. The world-view was mechanistic. In both the world of nature and that of man, each element was considered to be independent. The organic concept and the interdependence of functioning and support were still in the future. Therefore the leader was independent of the group. A good leader was considered to be effective with any group.

People did things because of the reward they received, or from fear of punishment if they did not. That is, motivation was apart from the task itself, or extrinsic. Persons felt their worth was judged by how well they performed. To be a good worker was almost synonymous with being a good man. The most widespread and influential idea was that of the survival of the fittest. Competition was accepted as the norm and viewed as almost an inherent quality of life. Such a view was supported by the research into animal life and the writings of Charles Darwin, especially *On the Origin of the Species.*[1]

By today's standards groups as part and parcel of these times left much to be desired. The interaction was restricted and restrained. It was seldom that members spoke to one another during the group session. They reacted only to the leader. The leader was the authority, the source of information and of planning and direction. The function of the members was to listen to the leader, to respect him and carry out his wishes. This kind of relationship ensured harmony and safety. Conformity was perceived as reasonable and good. The expert leader was the one who was efficient.

The format or seating arrangement of groups was planned to facilitate such procedure. Therefore the seats were in rows facing the leader. The leader was generally removed a few feet and frequently performed his function from behind a table or podium. He assumed that he knew what knowledge was needed by the members, that he could present it in such a way that they would understand it, that the members could and would assimilate it and relate it to previous information. To increase the possibility that they would make an effort to do so, some reward was extended such as praise, a grade, a certificate, a place of recognition in the group, or community recognition. Those who did not give attention (or who did and were unable to associate the ideas with their experience) felt failure and sometimes were punished in subtle or not quite so subtle ways. Listening was important but only listening to the leader to "get" the facts or ideas which he presented. These groups, of which there are numerous representations today, are generally identified as aggregate groups.

GROUPS IN THE EARLY 1900'S

The course of the future was changed by the dramatic insights of the last decade of the nineteenth and beginning of the present century. Instead of reliance upon authorities and ideas from the past, the acquiring of knowledge by direct observation and by the use of the scientific method became established. The individual gradually came into focus. More of his rights and privileges were recognized and each man came to be respected for his own ideas. Decisions were reached through the use of empirical evidence that was pertinent to the situation. The significance of the contribution of each informed citizen was recognized. The idea that all of those affected by the outcomes should have opportunity to participate in making the decision gradually gained acceptance.

This change from a mechanistic and authoritarian culture to an organic and cooperative one came about slowly. The first challenge to the mechanistic explanation came about through the work of Faraday and Oersted, which led to the insight of the magnetic field as a "field of force." The understanding of the field concept, that is, of the interrelationship of the field (environment) and the figure or figures (objects or persons) within it was advanced by insights from other fields. Auguste Comte, Herbert Spencer and Lester Frank Ward, through the direct study of society, provided substantial evidence of the field-figure relationships which came to be known as the study of sociology. Claude Bernard was able to elucidate the organismic role of the endocrine glands.

In the area of human relations, Charles Sanders Peirce, William James and John Dewey introduced ideas which have significantly affected interpersonal relationships even to the present day. In his *Collected Papers,* Peirce elucidated the components and their relationship in a psychological act. He gave first place to feeling, followed by action and thought. This placed feeling in a new relationship to thinking and acting as well as stressing their interdependent and integrated functioning.

Apparently there was little readiness to accept the significant part that feeling plays in all that we do. In any case John Dewey, a student of Peirce at Johns Hopkins University, chose to concentrate on thought as the focus of his attention. He made problem-solving thought the cornerstone of his study of behavioral change. He emphasized and demonstrated in his Laboratory School the importance of direct observation and experience. The impact of this method of learning had wide influence on education in all levels of endeavor. The concept of "learning by doing" was held by many in all walks of life. There was a growing urgency to transfer to humans the ideas of change and growth gained from experiments with animals. In so doing, man's capacity for human freedom, for doing the unexpected and seemingly impossible, was frequently neglected. In 1935 Dewey[2] called for an "organized cooperative inquiry" as a means of significant progress. Apparently he did not recognize that owing to the uniqueness of persons it is not possible to transcend conflicts of interest and achieve the intelligence he attributed to this process. Since then we have learned that persons and groups assert themselves in unpredictable ways, both good and bad. This is the mystery with which we must learn to live.

Charles Sanders Peirce ushered in a new way of looking at life and experience, which came to be known as pragmatism. In 1878 he made the claim that to develop the meaning of a thought it is only necessary to determine what conduct it is fitted to produce; the result is its sole significance.[3] The value of an idea or action is the result of how satisfactorily it works out for the person using it. William James, a student of Peirce, elaborated this new truth in an address in 1929. The new truth "makes itself true, gets itself classed as true by the way it works; grafting itself then upon the ancient body of truth which grows much as a tree grows by the activity of a new layer of cambium."[4]

Pragmatism, then, is first a method and second a generic theory. As a method it has given impetus to great scientific advancement. As a value system it has come under criticism. One psychologist comments as follows: "Pragmatism has provided a powerful stimulus to scientific study and practice. Indeed, it is the handmaiden of nearly all scientific endeavour. . . . Where pragmatism as a philosophy of life has its greatest drawbacks, however, is in the field of character and conduct. One can quickly sense the weakness of reducing the standard of right and wrong in this realm to mere expediency. . . ."[5]

Pragmatism has persistently become more influential since the beginning of this century. In the first two decades its effect was felt less, since it was still under the influence of religion. As a refined pragmatism it grafted itself onto religious and moral values, penetrating the vital tissues of the individual and society. As religion moved to the periphery of life and living for many, pragmatism's real nature was exposed. To those who could see, it was recognized as a "relatively uncontrolled philosophy of life in which expediency based upon ego-centric purposes guides the shifting destinies of the individual. Persons with this code cannot comprehend fair play, and are scarcely on speaking terms with duty, honor, courtesy, and other qualities which characterize the socialized individual. To them the man who does what is right because it is expected of him and because there are other people to be considered besides himself is an object of wonder." [6]

Such nation-shaping events quietly but significantly molded many individuals and groups. These events contained things useful and things questionable or even perhaps destructive. The turning away from tradition and from religious teaching as a guide to action divided the person in his loyalties and alienated him from habits, customs, and ways of acting and in turn from his recent friends. The Lynds[7] found that people felt unsure, were losing their bearings, did not trust their own judgment, and were less willing to trust the judgment of others.

During this period, the first half of our present century, attention focused on the small group as a means of solving problems. It was previously assumed that the individual could solve problems as well as or better than the group. Slowly it was accepted that group problem-solving could be superior. It was felt that this was most likely to occur when the necessity arose to develop and consider several possibilities.

A second trend was the assumption that decisions should be reached democratically. Although it was conceded that the leader should not make decisions for the group, many leaders in all walks of life considered the group members incapable of making decisions. Many of them, indeed, did not believe that employees, students and members of a family should even influence decision-making. In 1946 French, Kornhauser, and Morrow wrote: "Sometimes management is deliberately using the attractive symbols of democracy, participation, man-to-man discussion, group discussion, etc. to create the desired atmosphere within which it can smoothly manipulate the attitudes of its employees, retain their loyalty and still run the business 'as it should be run' without irritating influences from below." [8]

There was little member interaction in this atmosphere. Since the ideas of the members were not believed to be truly important, member-to-member communication was not encouraged. Members themselves seldom listened to one another but gave their full attention to the leader. Also since the purpose of the groups was to improve the outcomes of critical thought, little attention was given to any member's feeling about these outcomes. How the members felt about the group, one another, themselves or the leader was irrelevant to the main purpose of the group. The member's importance in and to the group was directly related to how he could perform. The church school classes and church groups in general were not true groups. Their usefulness was a function of the ideas they generated. The idea that these groups themselves should be examples of a Christian community was seldom recognized and then only to a limited degree. Many in leadership positions did not understand that a democratic leader had to be first a democratic person. Further, to learn how to share with the members only those tasks and plans for which they could assume joint responsibility was not easy. Many leaders became confused and misinterpreted the method as one in which they could withdraw from all leadership. The result frequently was some form of laissez-faire in which groups never developed any responsibility and did largely what they pleased.

The understanding of interpersonal relationships in groups also developed slowly. Although the organismic concept was widely accepted and discussed, it was only gradually understood. For instance, it was recognized that the person needed a variety of experiences just as an organ of the body needed a variety of foods. It was not recognized that these experiences must be assimilated and integrated in relation to the goals of the organism. Church schools and public schools provided numerous experiences or a varied curriculum which the curriculum planners viewed as comprehensive and interrelated but whose relationship and usefulness students were often at a loss to see.

Although the interrelationship and interdependence of functioning in the human body was becoming accepted fact, the application of this principle to human relations developed slowly. There was little recognition and feeling of belongingness and sense of responsibility for one another beyond the primary group. The increase of technological development and of greater mobility added to the feeling of separateness and the weakening of personal identity. The loss of feelings of personal adequacy militated against the progress of democratic functioning in groups. Members more easily submitted to the influence of leaders who were certain and had a plan.

GROUPS IN THE LAST TWO DECADES

By the close of the 1940's reason was no longer an inclusive concept which integrated feeling and thinking within a framework of values. Instead it had been put at the service of the fast-changing world of science. Reason now became technical reason in the service of the utilitarian and expedient, in relation to the threatening, shifting events at home and abroad. Increasingly man identified with the machine and the products produced. No longer did he consider himself the initiator, the maker, and the finisher of some product. He lost the symbol of himself as a creator and thereby lost his personhood. Like any product, he became an object for sale on the open market. His worth was in terms of what he could produce.

We turned increasingly to sources outside ourselves for meaning. Many persons became "joiners." They joined groups, clubs, and associations. David Riesman in his book, *The Lonely Crowd,*[9] describes the situation as a time when each person had, so to speak, a radar set fastened to his head to learn how to fit in. One person put it this way, "I'm just a collection of mirrors, reflecting what everyone else expects of me." On January 7, 1952, *Life* magazine carried an article entitled "The Wife Problem." The article summarized a series of researches which made the point that whether or not the husband was promoted depended on whether his wife as well as he fitted the "pattern" of the anticipated promotion.

Depersonalization triggered a sense of emptiness and loneliness. This was due to the growing and prevailing assumption that one was important for what he produced and also because of his exaggerated need to belong. One way to keep from being lonely was to engage in a whirl of social activities, to be in a group. Thus the idea of groups gained wide popularity. One must be a member of several groups: church, community and professional. A family which lived much of the time to itself came under suspicion, and the isolate in the classroom was considered to be seriously in need of help. To be different was a sure way of raising eyebrows. In accordance with the creeping influence of pragmatism, the means was not questioned. If the end state was the avoidance of loneliness, any means was accepted.

Groups in this era were in a transition period. But, looking back, one can say that so was society. In fact groups tended to lend themselves to superficiality. Members did not want to become truly involved with important matters. They were too apathetic and such matters would have been too threatening. In some ways, however, advances were made. Many people had experience in groups; they began to feel at home in them even though they were superficial. Groups were recognized as the format for getting many things done in industry, business, school and church. People of all ages were informally learning some of the skills necessary to group participation. Groups and cooperative planning went comfortably together. The vitality, capability and power of small groups gradually made themselves a force to be reckoned with in church, business, industry and schools.

GROUPS TODAY

Groups today are in the forefront of our thinking. Hardly any educational venture, whether in the field of medicine, law, industry or religion (to mention only a few), takes place without those involved spending part of the time in planned small group meetings.

Many of the popular journals regularly carry articles on small groups. This interest has accelerated greatly in the last decade. Ten years ago there were only scattered articles in journals and a few books. This increase in interest is the result of several factors, among them the psychological thrusts of a changing society, the changing place of religion, new insights and understandings regarding change in behavior, the search for meaning, the romantic thrust bringing in its wake an imbalance between feeling and thought, the confusion of emotion and feeling, a developing emphasis on the present combined with an anti-intellectualism and a contempt for the past, the cult of immediacy and the developing attitude of acceptance regarding impulsive behavior. All of these are clear indications that a new era is upon us.

The former sense of apathy and interest in conformity is fast disappearing. There is a new sense of optimism. The feeling of boredom is yielding to action. But this is a different kind of action. It is not action resulting from careful study and deliberation but the use of cohesive small groups acting impulsively, using any means at hand to force various segments of society to give them what they want. It is crude, unabashed pragmatism, which judges an action on the basis of outcome and is willing to justify any means to secure the desired result. Large segments of society are no longer willing to accept gradual change through innovation and trial and error. They want change now. They are not willing to take time to examine history to learn what is appropriate and how best to bring it about. Involvement, conflict, negativism, and force are the key methods in bringing change to pass.

These conditions have made possible the increasing popularity of the T group, and its offspring the encounter group, and the sensitivity group. These groups place much importance on immediate rather than gradual change, and also place heavy reliance on the emotions to induce change. They exemplify the influence of pragmatism in a striking manner in that the end is emphasized and the means to attain the end receive little attention. They expect and may encourage much conflict as a prerequisite to self-understanding and understanding of others in the group. As in all groups, they depend upon caring and a sense of responsibility to one another to effect positive results. Ambiguity, lack of structure, questioning and interpretation focused on the "here and now" experiences of the group are depended upon for genuine behavioral change in a constructive direction. The phrase "Tell it like it is" has become a shibboleth. It can be inferred that a clean break with the past is demanded. Tactful, considered, and considerate speech is less expected and to some degree less prized. The call is for open, honest confrontation. The assumption is that such confrontation will commence with the pouring forth of hostility and negativism. There is also a widespread conclusion that this is the only way significant change can take place.

While some conclude that genuine behavioral change takes place as a result of breaking down defenses and confronting one another with their inconsistencies and pretenses, others take a different view. These latter conclude that genuine change takes place when a person is free not to change. These theorists are interested in developing a group climate in which each person will feel safe and come to feel a sense of belonging as a member of the group. The assumption is that this permissive, safe, psychological climate will be conducive to expression of genuine concerns and feelings, self-chosen by the members.

This theory came to be known as self-theory and the method used as client-centered counseling with individuals and group-centered counseling with a group. Two of the many insights it emphasized were that intrinsic motivation is strong and dependable, and that the person himself is able to know more about himself than anyone else can. Although receiving little publicity, group-centered groups have functioned in all kinds of settings—church, school, industry and hospital.

The times, then, have engendered two distinct kinds of groups, the group-centered group and the T group. The group-centered group, beginning in the middle 1940's and reaching its zenith in the late 1950's and early 1960's, is now in the background. The T group, commencing in the late 1940's, remained in the background until the 1960's. In the 1960's and especially since 1965, it has come to occupy the center of the stage.

Each group is the outcome of many interdependent factors. Factors which aided one caused the other to recede. Some factors which aided the group-centered group were research by Kurt Lewin on behavioral change; emphasis placed on intrinsic motivation; genuine acceptance which encouraged a member to change. Members in such an environment chose to change constructively and began to do so; members had religious or moral values which operated as instigators in their choices of behaviors.

Factors which favored the developing popularity of the T group were loss of a personal center, alienation from self and others, insecurity, persons treated as objects, growing influence of pragmatism (end justifies the means), lack of interest and the incapability of many to become group-centered leaders, situational ethics, emphasis on immediacy, and emphasis on emotions as mediators of change. The method appealed to leaders in its satisfaction of ego needs. It did not require a leader to make any significant personality change in himself; authoritarian and pseudo-democratic types of leaders could succeed quite well. Other factors were a general lack of development of the depth potential of a large number of persons, the loss of religious values and the weakening of conscience. Self-expression to a large degree has, in such cases, superseded self-attachment to what is greater than the self. "What will I get out of life?" has usurped the question, "What will life, what will society, get out of me?"

Life in general, and interpersonal relationships in the group setting in particular, are influenced by the current trends. An examination of the trends listed below will help explain the method and activity in some of today's sensitivity groups.

1. The emphasis on emotion and feeling as the only necessary source of understanding.

2. The glorification of expression (open, frank, complete) as the road to a full, meaningful life and the neglect of dedication to something beyond self-interest.

3. The reliance upon the expedient, the utilitarian, the acting out, the values of the group (community, social group, work group, etc.) without the development of one's inner capacity for knowledge, valuation and decision.

4. The glorification of immediacy, the "here and now"; the impulsiveness of ephemeral emotional behavior and its confusion with the tested, deep and responsible way of relationship. Such confusion leads to error in the understanding of life's basic and enduring symbols such as love and peace.

5. The rootlessness of behavior, which is out of touch with the wisdom of the past and cut off from the promise of the future.

6. The neglect of the symbolic and the reduction of symbols to signs—love reduced to "doing your thing," peace to cessation of hostilities, the good life to freedom from pollution.

7. Immersion in the quicksand of the "it" world and removal from the solid ground of the I-Thou relationship.

8. The idolization of the idea of process and of limitless causation, on the one hand, and the loss of a personal center, on the other.

Thus it is not difficult to see how sensitivity groups fit the times. They are congruent with the trend and thought of many, but not all.

Current Issues of Self-Renewal in Group Process

The main issues in the use of group process formerly focused on its usefulness in the area of decision-making. Today, the focus has changed, although groups are widely used in the planning, carrying through, and evaluation of educational, scientific, and business endeavors. Issues currently revolve around the character and usefulness of groups in the encouragement of healthier interpersonal relationships in all areas of life. The key question has become, "Is group process a means of helping persons to enter into fuller, richer, and more meaningful living?" The issues bear a direct relationship to this concern.

A few of the chief issues have been selected for discussion here. They include the following: (1) How useful is the expression of one's personal concerns as a means of his personal growth? (2) What part does emotion play in self-examination and in changing individual behavior? (3) Are the kinds of decisions one makes and his relationships to others influenced by the depth at which he lives? (4) What are the ways in which persons are motivated to improve? (5) How do persons change their behavior?

These issues cannot be treated exhaustively in the space allotted. However, each presentation will offer insights and useful ideas concerning groups in relation to oneself.

IS VENTILATION ENOUGH?

If I tell the members of my group about my laxity in doing things on time, will I then commence to do them promptly? If I tell them about my action which hurt someone and which troubles me, will I be free of those twinges of guilt feeling? Can I have the assurance that I will not again do a similar wrong? If I tell them that I am hopeless and bored and just trying to get the days in, will life begin to have meaning again? These are serious questions of group members. They are asking, "Is ventilation enough?"

We would all like to have assurance that the trusting of oneself to the tender care of group members would mean a new life, a life of zest, purpose, and meaning, free from troublesome afterthoughts. The most optimistic response is that it could happen, but it is highly unlikely. The least optimistic response is that it is a start in the right direction. One may realistically conclude that it is worth doing and could initiate a change in the direction of becoming a more mature person.

However, it is possible for a member to tell about himself only because he desperately needs to be listened to, to feel he is worthy of attention. He feels no need to change and has no intention of committing himself to anything different. He does not sense a need to change but he enjoys being the center of attention.

One position developed by Carl Rogers and known as self-theory[10] takes what some may consider an optimistic view. It is assumed that if the leader and members are able to develop a climate in which the member feels unconditional acceptance, not only is he able to discuss his psychological problems and difficulties, but he will then begin to move in the direction of more fulfilling, constructive behavior. Such a conclusion is based on the belief that there is a built-in propensity called the "rationality of the organism" for moving toward self-fulfillment.

Kurt Lewin[11] takes the position that a member changes with the group. That is, he changes as the group changes and in the same direction. In this case as the members share their regrets and express their hopes for a better life, the group energizes itself as a group to move constructively.

Hobart Mowrer[12] also believes in the group's potential for change. However, he considers the possibilities for change greatly enhanced if the member in a group session conveys his sincere regret to those whom his actions have adversely affected. Mowrer considers the acceptance by those whom the member has harmed in a group setting a meaningful growth experience for everyone present.

Some group psychotherapists, among them Helen Durkin,[13] insist that ventilation is not sufficient, that insight and understanding of the relation of past events in one's life to his present functioning is necessary if more than superficial constructive change is to take place.

The crucial question is: What are the conditions which provide for the greatest assurance that members experiencing relief through oral expression will move forward to more mature growth-producing behavior? There is wide agreement that the possibility for growth is enhanced by the following conditions: (1) when the nature of the process used in the group can also be used in group situations in normal living; (2) the degree to which members can try out in the group itself new and developing patterns of behavior.

It is assumed that ventilation in some form is a prerequisite for behavioral change. There is no consensus that ventilation will necessarily or even generally usher in genuine and constructive behavioral change. It is necessary to recognize that we do not always respond to environmental conditions. We sometimes will do what seems impossible to others, and frequently we succeed. Sometimes what we will is for our own good and the good of others but at other times it is not. This human freedom that we have is part of our mystery. We must not idealize this, but on the other hand, we should never forget it.

WHAT OF THE EMOTIONS?

A second issue which is fast becoming a dilemma is the emphasis placed on emotions. We ask what function emotion ought to play in our decisions and behavior. The dynamics encouraged in some groups suggest that little that is useful can be expected to take place unless there is a high degree of emotional involvement. This may be one way in which groups reflect the times.

The pendulum has swung from an overemphasis on rational thought with a neglect of the emotions, to an overemphasis on the emotions without a corresponding emphasis on rational thought. Stated in an extreme manner, the movement has been from the assumption that learning or behavioral change took place without the necessary help of the emotions, to the assumption that learning or behavioral change needed the help of the emotions, and finally to the place that learning or behavioral change takes place because of the emotional involvement with only minimal need of rational thought. The overemphasis on emotions is increasingly apparent.

If Charles Sanders Peirce could return he would be surprised to find the disproportionate emphasis placed on emotions today. He placed emotions first in the psychology of the act, followed by action and thought. But it was an integrative concept which did not place importance on one to the almost total exclusion of the other.

A new and different emphasis came in 1950 in the writing of Samuel Beck. He wrote, "We cannot know without the intellect; we do not know until we experience with the emotions." [14] Until recently thinking processes were separated from emotional processes; and emotions were considered low on the scale of evolutionary development. They were frequently ignored or repressed. But it is now accepted that emotions and bodily drives arouse and energize thought.

Emotions are also credited with having specific directional qualities.[15] Fears among members in the group are considered to differ with each member's particular cause of the fear. The reactions to these fears are thought to be specific. Two members may behave very differently resulting from the fear that they will not be accepted. One may withdraw and say very little and the other may engage in much talking, often on subjects unrelated to the matter being discussed.

Even a cursory glance at the daily newspaper causes one to ponder the influence of emotions. Emotional drives operate at all levels of behavior from the most cognitive and sophisticated to the most natural and simple behavior. Also, emotional processes are considered to be perceptual. We react in terms of our perceptions. Perceptions of the group process, or the leader, or the participants account for the accompanying and individually different emotional reactions.

Some view the emphasis placed on emotions as a trend toward romanticism. Such a trend would mean a radical shift in our thinking about the nature of man. Instead of affirming his uniqueness to be his capacity for rational critical thought we are now asked to place increasing importance on his vitality (feeling, imagination and will).

This trend has made an impressive impact on the character of small groups. Forced into the background is the assumption that behavioral change results primarily from critical analysis and insight energized by the individual's desire to improve. Instead it is now increasingly assumed that high emotional involvement with others in relation to one another's present behavior is necessary for significant change to take place.

Such an assumption has led to the development of the T group and basic encounter groups. The leaders of these groups use various means to increase emotionality in relation to the "here and now" activity of the group. The expression of negativism, hostility and aggressive encounter with other members is frequently accepted as a necessary prelude to change.

As we return, then, to the question, "What of the emotions?" some tentative conclusions may be drawn. Emotion is necessary. It supplies energy and is also an important constituent of thought and action. Purpose and meaning deteriorate without emotion.

But emotion is like fire—a good servant but a poor master. Excessive emotion renders us incapable of thinking critically and acting wisely. To engender emotion for its own sake—that is, for an escape from boredom, for exhiliration, or for the purpose of conformity—is to misuse it. The outcome is always questionable and can be disastrous.

However, there is no virtue in remaining passive, stoic, unruffled or poised. Such behavior may be used to hide fear, to escape involvement, or to give an impression of stability. On the other hand, when emotions have full control, we may become thoughtless and irresponsible. Those who succeed in any useful endeavor usually feel emotion, but it is guided, disciplined and used to support the effort at hand. This is emotion rightly used.

The emotional norm differs from person to person. Not all individuals benefit from highly emotional interpersonal relationships. Each person joining a group should know to what degree the leader relies upon emotional effects to induce change in the members.

DEPTH OF INTROSPECTION

Do the decisions which members reach bear some relationship to their values and the depth of their introspection? It is common knowledge that we differ from one another in the way we reflect upon life and make decisions regarding our problems. Of course, some problems require a different consideration from others. Decisions which affect those for whom we have some responsibility should receive a depth of decision greater than other issues which do not involve us directly with people.

However, the fact remains that even in such situations

we differ widely. Some of us ask what would be most useful, most expedient, and/or most possible. On the other hand, some may ask first what is fair, what is just, and/or what is right? The outcomes of our decisions vary greatly in relation to the importance we place on each set of questions. It is easy to ask questions of utility, expediency, and possibility in trying to reach decisions, and often these questions suffice. However, in view of our personal responsibility, we need to ask questions of depth. To ask these questions means that we have established values and habits of subjecting our decision-making to the scrutiny of values and beliefs other than expediency.

Some of us develop our potential of asking ourselves both kinds of questions in our relationships with others. Such members are a blessing to the group. Their influence helps the group members to relate to one another at a more meaningful level, to share deeply and to trust one another.

The basic purpose of groups in some settings is to help one another to develop and use this depth dimension. The rush, turmoil, and ambiguity of modern living militate against this possibility. A time and place is needed when each (ideally assisted by others) inquires deeply about the meaning of life and his relation to others. The group provides this opportunity. Groups devoted to the deepening of interpersonal relationships and the building of a caring community develop within one the inwardness needed for dedication or rededication to living in accord with one's beliefs.

MOTIVATION

How familiar is the question, "Why do you suppose he did that?" The one who responds feels he cannot satisfactorily explain it either to himself or to his questioner. Down through the centuries we have offered explanations. These have changed with our changing knowledge of man and his behavior. Not too long ago, we concluded, workers could be encouraged to do more if they received more money. Now we believe that satisfying interpersonal relationships in small groups lead to greater output than just monetary recognition alone.

There was a saying, "Every man has his price." The assumption was that man's behavior could be controlled and directed by forces outside himself. Of course, this saying ignored the fact that many great leaders were great because they could not be induced by rewards or fear of rejection or punishment to conform to the demands of powerful others or conditions.

Pressures upon us coming from the environment or others in the form of rewards or losses or punishments have been described as extrinsic motivations. Educational systems, industry, business and the pattern of society itself are based on the theory of extrinsic motivation. Erich Fromm in his book *Escape from Freedom* describes our situation as the marketplace orientation. The importance of the person is in terms of what he can produce. He writes, "If there is no use for the qualities a person offers, he has none, just as an unsalable commodity is valueless although it may have its use value." [16]

Every day we hear examples of the use of extrinsic motivation. The teacher says, "That's a good answer, Bill." The counselor says, "You handled that situation well." A parent says, "I'm proud of your work in math." All of these are relying on a form of extrinsic motivation, generally called reinforcement. The reinforcer expects and hopes that his comments will encourage the person to continue or improve his performance. It is, however, based on two questionable assumptions—that the reinforcer knows the person sufficiently well to be able to judge the quality of his actions, and that he knows what is best for the person. This method may have succeeded in part since it does not require the one who is reinforced to establish his own goals or to assume responsibility for the results. If what he is encouraged to do does not succeed, he feels justified in placing responsibility on the one who encouraged him. It is also a source of ego-satisfaction for the reinforcer, especially when his reinforcements prove to be wise. When they fail, he generally resorts to rationalization.

Within the last decade a contrasting explanation of motivation has received increasing attention. Research has provided increasing evidence that intrinsic motivation may be a better explanation of why we do things. The claim is made that the difference between our goals and our perception of where we are motivates us to attain. Hunt,[17] known for his research on motivation, explains how intrinsic motivation works in the following manner. Using the room thermostat as an example he explains that the setting of the thermostat is the standard or goal, the room temperature the input, and the difference in the reading between the setting (goal) and the room temperature (input) the incongruity that instigates the operation, or that which causes us to "get going." Each person has his standard or standards. They can lead either to progressive (more mature) or regressive (less mature) behavior. There are many kinds of standards in relation to our values, our beliefs, and the different areas of our lives.

A crucial issue in groups today is the choice between the use of extrinsic or intrinsic motivation. Some groups rely on the first, some on the second, and some on a combination of the two. The authoritarian group relies on extrinsic motivation; the democratic and group-centered on intrinsic, and the T group, basic encounter, and sensitivity groups on some combination of extrinsic and intrinsic motivation. Since the theories and methods of motivation are based on contrasting views of behavior and behavioral change, there are conflicting inconsistencies within groups which depend on a combination of both methods of motivation. Leaders in groups which depend on extrinsic motivation depend upon one or more methods of reinforcement—interpretations, questions, interventions, suggestions. Leaders of groups who depend on intrinsic motivation depend upon unconditional acceptance of members, clarification of members' comments, reflection of meaning, linking ideas for members to make the thinking clear, and summarizing when necessary. Leaders (trainers) of T groups use both extrinsic and intrinsic methods of motivation, such as interpretation and acceptance, evaluation of comments and clarification, permissiveness and interventions (interrupting discussion to explain what is happening in the group). It should be noted, however, that acceptance is not unconditional. It is acceptance only within the framework set by the trainer in relation to his goals and the current objectives he has for the process.

All groups depend upon a caring, responsible relationship as a necessity for members to receive constructive help. The issue finally becomes which method furthers the dignity and personhood of the member and induces his participation to the degree that he engages in self-examination, gains self-understanding and resets constructive goals for himself.

The present conclusion is that no particular group method motivates all members to the same degree. Some people are helped by one method; others are helped by a very different method. At present we are at a loss to know in advance which kind of group is best for any member.

HOW DEVELOP A LOVING CONCERN?

Group leaders endorse a loving concern as the necessary condition for meaningful growth relationships in the group.

A loving concern is assumed to be the end product of widely different conditions. The leader may use praise and encouragement, or he may question or reject certain expressions; that is, he may reinforce in order to encourage certain responses and attitudes. This can easily become thinly masked manipulation. He may purposely develop an ambiguous situation in which the members do not know for sure what is expected or what to expect. He may do this to encourage the expression of strong feeling, often hostile and negative. He may assume that the expression of such feeling is a prerequisite for more positive relationships. In other groups there is a real unconditional acceptance of each member leading hopefully to the trust of each member in the others. Regardless of the kinds of interpersonal relationships during the major life of groups all depend in the end on a condition of genuine loving concern as the curative and fulfilling emergent in group process.

Part of the issue revolves around the understanding of love itself, and additionally, around what conditions in the group encourage the state of loving concern. The question is often asked: Can a small group of persons over a weekend, a week, or two weeks really come to love one another? Some persons answer in the affirmative. Others express serious doubts, claiming that a longer time, free from external pressure to love, is necessary.

This remains an issue. Trainers in sensitivity groups and basic encounter groups believe this is possible and that it does occur. Others say that for the majority it is pseudo-caring. They claim that appearances may be deceiving.

One criterion for deciding the quality of love in a situation is the degree to which creative risk is basic to the undertaking. Misrepresentations of love take many forms. Three of these forms will be discussed.

Some members assume that there is a standard of conduct which must be adhered to under all conditions. These standards may come from many sources but they are not to be questioned. In fact they reveal in themselves the essence of love. For these members what is "right" and "good" is confused with what is "correct." A member then believes he is loving when he does what is normative or "correct" in the situation. To love does not mean a relationship but only the doing of what is proper and correct. Such a member acts as if he cares about and loves other members because he perceives that this is what is expected. These members ask, "What should I do? What is expected?"

Other members differ from these in that they have no dependable guides or principles. They do not see or attempt to see any connection between the several threads of experience. They do not expect or try to discover relationships. Their actions tend to be spontaneous and irregular. They illustrate the cult of immediacy. For them love is ephemeral, emotive, and reduced to the wholly psychic, subjective level of feeling. These members ask, "What am I to do?"

A third group does not make use of the past in trying to understand reality. They do not recognize any relationship between a person making a decision and the situation in which he has to make it. It is as if the situation is suddenly flashed on the screen of their experience. It is a ready-made, a simple "That's how it is." Time relationships past, present and future do not exist; it is just "the case." For these members there is only the question: What do I want out of it?

For the three types of members just described the experience of love in the group is nonexistent. Love is not something which can be turned on and off.[18] You don't start to love because it is expected, or because it appears to be the better alternative or for what you can get out of it. Love is basic, a given desire for union. We can't schedule it, we can only prepare the conditions which may encourage it.

The forms of loving described above do not encourage the conditions conducive to true caring. These members are hardly likely to benefit genuinely or to change because of the group experience. This may be especially the case if they feel under pressure from members or from the leader to react emotionally. Since this kind of involvement is part of the T-group and basic-encounter-group experience, pseudo or false expressions of caring may result.

In T groups those members who lack a personal center[19] and dedication to personal values may be forced into pretense in order to conform and reduce the threat they feel. Those who do have a personal center and know their values and beliefs do not need the experience as much. They may, however, be able to help others in their self-exploration.

In group-centered groups each is free to be what he feels he really is. The permissive climate induces genuineness and the movement toward caring and responsibility develops slowly but is part of the members' total developmental change. However, some members may avoid self-confrontation and may not fully use the experience to develop understanding and caring for other members.

All group leaders hope to develop a loving concern of one member for another. In doing so they make contrasting assumptions concerning the necessary conditions. T group leaders use ambiguity, interpretation, and limited acceptance especially in the initial stages, increasing their acceptance and diminishing their interventions in the last stages. Group-centered leaders use unconditional acceptance, clarification and reflection. In each kind of group some members benefit. In both groups some benefit much more than others, and a minority do not benefit; a few may even regress.

The Possibilities of Self-Renewal

History is a record of what groups may accomplish. Groups have molded history for better or for worse since the beginning of time. We can agree that the group approach has possibilities. The focus of concern becomes "possibilities for what?" The more information and experience we gain, the more involved the answer becomes.

Our whole perspective changed as we recognized the implications of the organismic approach as an explanation of the possible interdependence of functioning among the members. Previous to this we had doubts that a group could solve problems more efficiently than the individual. We were also skeptical that the group experience was a possible means of growth. Many saw the individual losing his freedom, becoming more dependent and conforming. The fact that members of a group could be different from one another and share their differences constructively was considered impossible.

Such doubts, skepticism and unbelief were the outcomes of misjudgment concerning the functioning of the leader and members. The failure to apply organismic principles to group functioning forced the skeptical into a mechanistic, authoritarian mode of explanation.

What, then, is the concept which has so radically changed our conception of the group and its possibilities? Hopkins describes this concept as the organic group, or a number of individuals working together in a process of meaningful interaction which releases in them a latent emergent quality of wholeness previously unknown to any individual.[20]

The name "organic" is given to this kind of group because individual members function in a similar dynamic relation to each other and to the whole, as do the various organs of the body to each other and to the whole. That is, each member ideally functions in a manner similar to the functioning of the organs of the body. Let us examine this functioning. (1) We recognize that each organ has a specialized function to perform for the good of the whole. (2) This specialized ability and function is recognized and respected by all others (the nose does not try to take over the function of the ears). (3) The organism as a whole recognizes that it cannot maintain itself without the specialized functioning of the parts. (4) Any one function of the parts is not placed on a higher level than another. One is not favored over another. (5) When some part is temporarily unable to perform its services, thereby threatening the integrity of the whole, other organs stimulate the sluggish one to a normal performance or devise means of taking care of its duties.

This is the highest cooperative process known. Each organ remains sensitive to the others at all times. Leadership moves from organ to organ depending upon the need of the whole.

The implications of this concept of organismic functioning help explain the possibilities of the group. In such a group there is interdependence and respect. Each member is a part of the group regardless of how he functions. Each depends on the functioning of every other, and each accepts the others and trusts that they will add to the health of the group. Leadership moves from member to member in relation to the particular needs of the group at the time and the capability of the member to assist. All the planning and decisions are made by the group itself. Decisions are reached by consensus. Consensus means that every member recognizes and assents to the fitness of the judgment or action to achieve the purposes which are commonly accepted.

The possibilities of the group for constructive psychological growth of the members and improvement in decision-making bear a direct relationship to the degree to which they function as an organic group.

Groups vary greatly in their possibilities of helping members. It is possible that members may not be helped in a group, and a small percentage may even be harmed. Questionable groups are those in which members feel threatened, are treated as objects, or are pressured to conform in some degree to the wishes of other members and/or the leader. Because of our individual differences, it is unrealistic to expect any group to help everyone. On the other hand, some people may be helped in almost any group. To assume that every person needs to have the experience of being a member of a group has not been justified.

Today, small groups are man's best hope for greater self-understanding and understanding of others. In addition to this, small groups can act as a strong change catalyst in many kinds of organizations and institutions. There are some things which happen in a group which are unlikely to take place outside of it. Let us look at some of these.

The meaning of each member's experience is in large part a function of his perceptions. Each brings his own unique way of relating to others, his own fears and his particular skills of communication. Those who bring much self-concern, feelings of inadequacy, and a hesitancy to let themselves be known and to know others commence at a different point from those who are almost free of these hindrances. Each member moves in the same general direction, but the rate of change varies from member to member.

The group holds possibilities for growth for all of these. These possibilities are of several kinds. The member gradually feels differently about himself; he perceives himself as a necessary part of a group; his feeling of adequacy improves; he feels he is worthy and worthwhile. He gains respect for himself; he becomes more able to contribute in the group. His listening improves; he becomes able to hear what members are saying; his powers of concentration improve; he can follow the ideas of other members and consider them. He feels that he is acceptable as he is; he becomes more interested in the members and begins to accept responsibility for the general progress of the group and for helping individual members. Briefly stated, his feeling about himself—his self-image—improves. He improves in his understanding of others. He develops his skills for communication. He develops his sense of responsibility.

It should be cautioned that not all groups provide such possibilities for becoming a person. Groups differ widely in their purposes and methods. These wide differences are a function of the leader's behavior with reference to both his perception of what a group should be and his own ego needs. The leader who feels it necessary to have the dynamics of the group revolve around him develops and maintains one kind of psychological climate. Other leaders who satisfy their ego needs through their recognition of seeing the members develop and who relate more freely and take more initiative develop a very different psychological climate. It would be well for the individual to know the thinking of the leader concerning groups before becoming a member. The label given to the proposed group experience generally does not offer much help to the prospective member.

Coffey[21] describes a group situation which was disappointing to the members because of the leader's confusion resulting from his own lack of theory and the members' dissatisfaction with the method used. In one case a staff desired acquaintance with group procedures in order to improve their staff functioning. The leader misinterpreted their interest and viewed the group as asking for a therapeutic experience. Instead of helping the members consider content and the direction they might take for improvement, he concentrated upon the release of negative and hostile feelings.

Members in the group process need to know what the leader plans to do and what is expected of them. Then they need to use their imagination to sense how they might feel in the group. It is best that one not join a group until he has explored its purposes and methods.

Groups, then, have two distinct possibilities. The experience can assist members in becoming persons and in the development of skills which aid them in their interpersonal relationships. They are assisted in becoming persons through self-understanding and understanding of others. With reference to themselves they clarify their goals, learn of the ways in which they tend to satisfy their ego demands and to some degree come to know why they behave as they do. In turn they recognize that others have reasons for what they do. They begin to understand why other members act as they do and sense the meaning of interdependence and of responsibility. They develop skills of listening, of clarifying ideas for others and themselves, of reflecting the meaning of what is expressed, of following the threads of thought, and of linking ideas together and summarizing. Whereas before the experience they became lost in the flow of ideas, they now become able to follow the ideas expressed and to relate one to another.

Of course the group experience has to some degree different possibilities for different members. For those who seldom introspect, it provides an opportunity and encouragement to do so. Those who customarily examine their purposes and actions become able to do so more comprehensively and more easily. Not only does the experience encourage more looking at oneself, but it promotes the doing of this at a greater depth. Where formerly one asked chiefly the questions of expediency, the what and how, he now asks the questions of rightness, the why, questions of the justice, the fairness, the worthiness of the alternative plans of action in relation to his values and beliefs. The experience clarifies and emphasizes the interdependence each shares with others in day-to-day living and the need to be dependable and responsible.

Leaders and members who have predetermined goals and manipulate one another toward achieving them treat themselves and others as objects. In such instances the value of the experience becomes questionable. But when persons remain more important than plans and what happens to them as individuals remains paramount, the group experience has constructive possibilities.

2 THE NATURE OF THE SMALL GROUP

What Is a Group?

MISCONCEPTIONS

The various ways in which the word "group" is used lead to some unfortunate misconceptions. Quite often we hear the suggestion, "Let's use small groups." It is generally a good idea, for often more may be accomplished in this way than through the lecture format. However, a collection of people does not immediately become a group. They may become a group if they meet regularly over a period of time with the assistance of a trained leader.

Another misconception is that the saying, "We had a good discussion" is the same as saying, "We had a good group." In a "good group" there is generally "good discussion," but a "good discussion" may take place without the participants having become a "good group." There is a qualitative and symbolic difference between a discussion group and a true group.

A few people in a face-to-face situation may seem to be a group when actually they have only the outward appearance of one. Such appearance may be compared to a fine-looking car which lacks a motor. The attainment of difficult skills and considerable "becoming" are necessary in order for a collection of people to assist in the development of a group and in the improvement of its function.

ELEMENTS OF A DESCRIPTION

The nature of the group is complex. No one definition is adequate. Instead, authorities try to describe it, each one emphasizing the aspect which seems most important to him. Kurt Lewin and others used the interdependence of members as a criterion. Krech and Crutchfield accept this description and elaborate it as follows: "A group refers to two or more people who bear an explicit psychological relationship to one another." [1] In other words, each is related to others in such a way that the behavior and characteristics of others influence him. Cattell describes the group as referring to "two or more organisms interacting in the pursuit of a common goal in such a way that the existence of many is utilized for the satisfaction of some needs of each." [2] Also each member remains in contact with all the others, with an open readiness to modify his ideas and attitudes as his perceptions change. In fact, the dynamics frequently overlooked are the willingness of each member to listen, to try to understand, to consider a statement from another on its merits, and to draw conclusions based on the evidence presented rather than solely on preformed values.

On the operational level, a group is composed of two or more persons in an interdependent psychological relationship. They pursue a common goal through interaction with one another and the leader. They are willing to modify their ideas and actions.

On the qualitative and symbolic level, the high degree of interpersonal responsiveness is based on the satisfaction of some needs, caring, and a sense of responsibility. Each member, through his experiences in the group, comes to a realization that he is accepted regardless of what he produces. The presence of these characteristics in the individual members of the group makes it possible for the people to communicate genuinely in depth.

A group cannot be adequately described. It is different from the sum of all that goes into it. The depth of feeling and the sense of "becoming" have to be experienced to be understood.

Organization and Maintenance of Groups

DIFFERENCES AMONG SMALL GROUPS

Groups differ widely in their organization. They differ in the kind of leadership and the structure.

Groups are formed for different purposes. Some groups are interest groups, some are planning groups, some study groups; some are for the training of leadership, and some are for understanding and spiritual renewal. The ideal is the involvement of persons from various age groups. The most interesting groups to the members themselves are composed of persons who are very different from one another, both with reference to age and sex, and in terms of their educational and work experience. Although there will be age groups discussing ideas and engaging in activities peculiar to the interests and purposes of the age, there will also be groups composed of youths, young adults, and older persons. Such groups will help to diminish the fancied and real barriers between the generations. Such multi-age and -interest groups assure wider interest and increased understanding of one another. They also encourage respect for ideas past and present and cooperation in putting into effect plans made by the group.

METHODS OF GROUP FORMATION

Groups may form themselves or be formed in various ways. A number of people may come together because of their interest in a topic to be studied. They divide themselves into small groups of five, seven, or nine persons, depending upon the number of leaders available to meet with the groups.

In some instances, one experienced leader may assist a number of groups. These will meet in the same room. For instance, thirty people may meet in three groups of approximately ten each. Meeting one night a week for two hours each evening, they will spend part of the time in a total group of thirty led by the trained leader, and part of the time in small groups of ten each, with the leader spending one period with one group and moving to another group for a second period. They may spend forty minutes in a small group and thirty minutes in the total group, at which time reports are heard and plans are made for the final small-group meeting. Ten minutes may be allowed for a break after the first or second time module.

The break is an important part of a full-length meeting. It provides a change of pace and allows members to mingle and relate informally. Social behavior has important elements somewhat different from the behavior of the formal group. The leader will be interested in the increasing amount of interchange among members and the relaxed atmosphere.

Groups may be formed in different ways and for many purposes. To illustrate this, let us use relationships in the church community: (1) a few persons interested in a study of the liturgy of the church or the furthering of ecumenicity within the church may contact a few others of like mind and form a group; (2) an official of the church may appoint a group for a certain purpose; (3) a number of persons may be invited by the religious educator to train as group leaders who would then be available to lead other groups in the church; (4) an elected official body composed of church members may invite a trained leader to assist them in using group process in their discussions and decision-making; (5) several small groups may work both separately and interdependently in the preparation for a banquet, a social event, or a play.

Regardless of how the groups are formed, members need the freedom to develop and use their own ideas and to work out their own process and plans. Groups need to be related to some general aspect of Christian life in the church itself or beyond. They need to be recognized by the official board of the church and should have a regular avenue for reporting to this board.

Groups differ with different methods of leadership. These methods require different degrees and kinds of structure. T-group and basic-encounter-group leaders depend upon lack of structure, ambiguity, and some frustration as initial means of increasing members' involvement. Democratic and group-centered leaders supply some initial structure as a means of making members feel comfortable and safe. They consider this a prerequisite for necessary involvement of the members in the process.

Leaders of T groups and of similar groups also remain psychologically apart from the group and intervene only to induce greater involvement and to give direction to the discussion. Democratic and group-centered leaders are special members of the group from the beginning. As such, they do not intervene by making interpretations or suggesting the direction the members should take. They are interested in the progress of the group and they assist members in the evaluation of the process and in making plans. They do this during the discussion if the member leading the group requests it. The chief evaluation on which the group depends for insights occurs at the close of the discussion in a permissive and accepting way.

MAINTENANCE OF GROUPS

The maintenance or ongoingness of the group depends upon the degree to which the experience satisfies individual and group needs. These needs vary from member to member. Members need to feel that they are respected and accepted by other members. They also need to feel that they are necessary to the group. A feeling that one "belongs" encourages interest and cooperation. Members need to experience the trust of other members in order to trust and share themselves with others.

Members have other needs besides those concerning personal adequacy and interpersonal relatedness. They have intellectual needs; that is, needs to examine experience, to learn, and to know. This learning and knowing is not only related to the content of the subject under discussion but is the need for each person to learn about himself and to understand himself and others in relation to the subject and the general progress of the group.

These needs are satisfied in several ways. Some leaders ask each member to write a "self-report" at the close of the meeting. In this report each person describes how he feels about the group experience for that meeting. Also each member indicates ways in which he hopes to change in future meetings. These reports are anonymous, being identified by number only, and are returned by the leader after a number of meetings to the members for review. At this time the leader also reviews the reports, including his own self-report, in order better to understand the members and himself.

Members elect from their number an observer for each meeting, thus rotating the position among themselves. The observer sits with the members in the circle. He may participate as a member but frequently does so only occasionally in order to give his attention to what is happening in the group. The observer concentrates on such matters as participation (who participates and how frequently), how well the members listen to one another, and whether or not they are focusing on the topic they have chosen and are treating it in depth. The observer tries to indicate how well members are sharing the time, and whether they are "hedging" or giving their feelings and ideas full rein. He also observes the leader. Is the leader facilitating the discussion? Does he clarify ideas which are not clear? Does he reflect the meaning of statements? Does he help members to make a transition to other aspects of the subject?

The observer reports during the discussion, if requested to do so by the leader, and also at the close of the session. The group members depend upon his comments to help them understand what has taken place. The leader also comments on his own leadership. He explains what he hoped to do, what he did do, and what he would try to do if he were doing it again. The members report on the difficulties they experienced, what was helpful to them and what they plan to do in the future.

Occasionally the members ask the observer to note certain things and to report on them. They also recognize what skills they are using and plan to improve and broaden their ways of functioning in the group. They are usually surprised to note that they are accustomed to using only two skills—giving information and asking questions.

Comparison of Educational, Counseling, and Therapy Groups

The various forms of groups are on a continuum. Each has some of the elements of all the others. No kind of group is completely different from another. In order to understand them correctly, it is necessary to classify them and consider the commonalities and differences of each classification. The attributives, such as democratic, group-centered, analytic, T group, basic encounter, and sensitivity may indicate to some degree the method, but in no wise do they indicate the function. In other words, any or all of these methods may be used for education, counseling or therapy.

Hence, three broad, descriptive classifications have been chosen: educational groups, group counseling, and group therapy. A description of each of these follows:

EDUCATIONAL GROUPS

These groups have specific goals. These goals are often the attainment of such end products as the completion of plans for a program, a party, or a unit of study. In addition, the group may establish other goals at the beginning of the process or during it, such as knowledge of content (if it is a course or unit of study), development of skills and increased self-understanding.

In these groups critical thinking is focused maximally on ideas and minimally on emotional problems. Knowledge and know-how from the past are focused on understanding and doing something about the problems of the present, the "here and now" of the group process. There is the achievement of skills as well as some improvement in self-understanding and understanding of others.

The leader assists the members in recognizing and experiencing the nature of an "organic" group. This results in increasing permissiveness and acceptance among the members. Each comes to understand and accept the fact that his membership is not dependent upon what he produces. He realizes that he is not in a competitive situation and that he is a member and a person in his own right. The members also discover that their ideas are considered genuine and significant expressions.

As the members develop an increasing sense of responsibility for the process and for assisting one another, the leader moves to the periphery and his ideas are considered and discussed like those of other members. As the leader loses his traditional image of director, minister or supervisor (depending upon the situation), the members' feeling of adequacy develops and participation becomes easier and more spontaneous. This is assisted by the leader's increasing awareness that a useful discussion can take place without following his preplanned outline. He becomes more confident of the adequacy of the members in carrying the discussion forward and more willing and able to remain in the background as a facilitator.

Members of the group become involved as a result of several conditions. The absence of extrinsic evaluation causes each to re-examine continually his process, ideas and contributions. The discussion of process by the leader encourages introspection and the resetting of levels of aspiration. This results in direct contact with others and their ideas, identification with the feelings of others, and a developing sense of responsibility, belongingness and adequacy.

Reality testing, which is an integral part of group process, occurs in several contexts. The member is testing the old and new attitudes toward education. The novel aspects implied in the discussion of permissiveness, support and stimulation are conducive to the member's development of new insights into his own attitudes and those of others. He tests his attitudes, behavior, responses and ideas on the spot. He uses the results of his testing in his future relationships in the group, and he transfers those which prove adequate to life outside the group setting. The leader tests his methods against what he believes about behavioral change. He also checks for congruence. Is he doing what is in accord with his feelings and beliefs about the dignity of persons? And finally, are the methods he is using securing the anticipated results?

GROUP COUNSELING

Members who have participated in educational groups move easily into the necessary interpersonal interaction of group counseling. Experience in groups helps to develop the needed skills and a sense of responsibility for the welfare of other members and for the functioning of the group process in general.

The goals in group counseling cannot be easily verbalized or visualized but are generally understood to be the satisfaction of emotional needs. Problem-solving is only incidentally related to ideational situations and instead focuses on the understanding of emotions and the resolving of emotional conflicts. Critical thinking is focused on the emotional content of interpersonal and intrapersonal relationship. It is concentrated frequently on the "here and now" that is occurring in the group at the time. Occasional decision-making occurs in relation to self-understanding and the understanding of others.

A high degree of permissiveness is present, which is accompanied by a deep level of emotional involvement. This permissiveness increases the safety of the group situation and its unrestricted choice of what is to be discussed. Emphasis is on acceptance and understanding. Mutual support increases the possibility of discussion of the meaningful problems of the members. Creative differences in values, ideas and feelings are expected and accepted.

The ability and readiness to share oneself with others

broadens and deepens in such a climate. Members sense a deep relatedness as they discover that others have some of the same problems that they have. They find that others will listen and try to understand them and their ideas and problems.

Motivation stems from various sources. Some arises from interest in the problem being discussed. It is furthered by the interaction and the expression of contrasting and different viewpoints. As in educational groups, there is an integral relationship between what takes place within and outside the group. This is evidenced in the ideas discussed and plans made which are put into effect immediately. There is the additional stimulation of experimentation in the counseling group. Here the members experiment together with attitudes, ideas, and solutions in order to learn the degree of possibility and workability of these ideas and attitudes. There is, therefore, a greater degree of isolation between the group's concern and the outside world. This degree of isolation is necessary at times in order to facilitate the concentration upon personal emotions and their examination. In educational groups, the movement is back and forth between the practice aspect, planning, decision-making, evaluation, and the action phase, i.e., putting plans into action. But in group counseling the action phase receives more emphasis, i.e., experimentation with group members' ideas, emotions and attitudes, followed by generalizations which become active in the outside world.

There is acceptance of a wide range of attitudes and ideas. This encourages each member to describe and examine his problems. He is free to introduce his concerns and he assumes responsibility for doing so. Thus each member's expressions tend to be meaningful and genuine. Each member who discusses his problems is encouraging others to do so.

As a feeling of ease develops in a free, give-and-take atmosphere, there is added warmth and spontaneity. Also, the discussion of attitudes and emotions has a natural relationship to the topic under consideration and is handled with sufficient ease and clarity to contribute to the member's understanding.

The experience prompts each member as a matter of course to test his attitudes and ideas against reality. He is interested in knowing if his ideas are acceptable and useful and if his attitudes are indicative of the kind of person he wishes to become. In his reality-testing he projects his conclusions beyond the group to the world in which he expects to live in order to gauge their suitability and acceptability. His reality-testing differs from that of those in educational groups. The difference revolves around his search for who he is and what has personal meaning for him and not just the determination of the practicality of ideas and plans.

GROUP THERAPY

Unlike group counseling, which is for members who are functioning normally, group therapy is designed to help those who suffer from minor reactions to situational stress and those who have severe neurotic disturbances and psychoses. Some in therapy seek help on their own, while others are referred by counselors, medical practitioners or psychiatrists. Therapists differ widely in their goals and procedures. Regardless of their orientation, all therapists desire to free the patient's spontaneity and capacity for emotional growth so that he may become more comfortable, effective and emotionally mature.

Permissiveness is essential in group therapy. The therapist considers it part of the therapy. His own attitude and the evident safety of the group lend relief to individual members. The therapist is supportive but in a different way from much of the support of leaders in other groups. His support is selective and used to reinforce certain attitudes and behaviors. He uses it especially to reduce the annihilating loss of self-confidence suffered by many members.

The members are more strongly motivated than those in other groups. They desire to get well. Many suffer from internalized controls in the form of guilt feelings and fear of criticism. Further stimulation arises from antagonisms due to conflicting values, rivalry for the therapist's attention, association with the problems of others, perception of the progress another member is making and the direct contagion of the situation.

Reality-testing is a very important aspect. It is more difficult since the member is in great need of the security of his group world to help him in carrying through. The member evaluates himself by the acceptance he receives from the group. This procedure helps him to understand the other members and himself. One important means of realistically appraising himself is to try out his ideas and feelings in the group. The other members and the therapist help him to examine these and make some conclusions. The relative directness and forthrightness of members' reactions help each one to see how his behavior is perceived by others. He projects his new concepts into relationships in the outside world and determines whether or not they will be acceptable.

3 *GROUP PATTERNS*

The Authoritarian Group

The authoritarian group[1] has the longest tradition and is the most common. It is slowly yielding to those groups whose method makes use of the interdependence of relationships as they exist in our organic world.

Authoritarian groups encompass all the purposes established for small groups. As educational groups they are organized to secure ideas and make decisions. As in counseling and therapy groups, the purposes range from solving personal problems and preventive hygiene to significant personality and behavioral change.

PATTERNS OF USE

The authoritarian method is used in a multitude of settings in church, business, industry, family, psychological clinics, counseling bureaus and government. In the church it is frequently the basic method for official boards, committees, educational groups, leadership-training groups and recreational groups.

The authoritarian process, then, takes many forms of expression and claims, as it should, its fair share of usefulness in multiple settings. It is unfortunate that many of those who use it hesitate to name it correctly. They apparently prefer to view their leadership as democratic. The pseudo-democracy which results is unjust to both authoritarianism and democracy. A wiser and more honest procedure would be to assert that it is authoritarian and gradually change toward the democratic if and when it is desirable to do so. It is common knowledge that management in church, business and industry deliberately uses the attractive symbols of democracy, participation, man-to-man discussion or group discussion in order to create the desired atmosphere in which it hopes to retain loyalty and manipulate attitudes toward management's desired goals. Such procedures have been a deterrent in understanding the advantages and weaknesses of both authoritarian and democratic groups.

PROCESS

The members generally sit in rows facing the leader. This is a logical arrangement, since it is only a two-way process. The leader speaks to the members and the members speak to the leader. Members sometimes sit in a horseshoe or circle arrangement, an innovation of recent times. The interaction, however, does not change.

The status leader is appointed from without the group because he is an expert in the subject. He assumes responsibility for the leadership of the members. He plans the content, decides the methods, the times of presentation, and the rewards or punishments to be used. He presents the content which he believes the learner should know in lecture form, or by other media such as maps, charts, films, tapes, etc. He may also use discussion as a means of leading the members to his predetermined conclusions.

He relies on increasing quantities of information as the means of improving the experience of others. The information is taken from books and other sources on an ascending scale of critical thinking or psychological difficulty.

LEADERSHIP

The authoritarian leader assumes that his knowledge and decisions are superior to those of the group. He thus perceives his function to be one of directing the members toward predetermined goals. He plans for the group by setting forth its purposes, objectives and the methods to be used in attaining them. He uses lectures, explanations and directions. He directs the group through evaluative comments, interpretations, suggestions and interventions in the process. He hopes to assure the direction and the outcomes of the group. By such procedure he centers control in himself.

He expects a high degree of conformity, since he assumes that the group is inexperienced, untrained and unintelligent about the problem or even incapable of dealing with it alone.

A good authoritarian leader is forceful and energetic, an expert planner and organizer. He is firm, kind and successful in securing the cooperation of the members.

MEMBERSHIP

Members perceive their function as one of understanding the ideas and demands of the leader, and use much psychic energy in determining them. Their response to the situation varies in accordance with their past experiences and their openness to new experiences. Some of the members welcome the security provided through the structure. They cooperate and relinquish their right to make decisions regarding their involvement in exchange for the rewards which result from good behavior. They also relinquish to the leader the responsibility for the success of the enterprise. In the church group this may mean that members attend irregularly if the leader fails to interest them. Some take a cooperative stance or react with passivity, conformity, withdrawal, or "apple-polishing."

Others may react differently. They dislike sacrificing their right to share in the plans and decisions regarding the group and may as a consequence restrict their response, or sabotage the plans, suggestions or requirements set forth by the leader. A few, unable or unwilling to control their displeasure, may project their negative feelings on other members, on the leader, or on the prescribed conditions. Counterhostility may result, or cliques may form which undermine the leader's authority.

Members in an authoritarian group are unlikely to develop much sense of responsibility or caring for one another. Each member is an object to the others, a means of making possible the satisfaction of his own needs. The lack of trust in one another is not helpful to the development of a psychological climate conducive to mental health.

THEORETICAL BASIS

Authoritarian leadership is based upon association theories of learning. The assumption is that one learns by associating a learned idea with a new idea, noting similarities and differences, or by associating one object with another, or one individual with another. Primarily attention is focused upon the relation between individuals and objects. The associationist takes an external objective approach to behavior. The behavior of a group member is considered to be a function of the externally controlled stimulus. The center of the member's learning experience is not inside him. It is outside and in those things in the environment which can be measured. Change in the behavior is the result of learning the connections and interrelationships which exist in the conditions outside the learner. These he learns from authority figures, ministers, directors of religious education, teachers, employers and others. Change in the thinking, feeling and acting of the individual or group is directed by ideas, meanings and values which are inserted into the psychological field by authorities at the outset to control behavior. The function of evaluation resides in the authority figure and the individual group member uses psychic energy in trying to discern and to move in a praiseworthy direction.

Each member is considered separate but not unique. He is expected to be motivated by the leader and to conform. Variability in ideas and behavior is unwelcome. The member is conditioned to feel adequate and worthy only if the leader indicates that he perceives him as such. The member tends to relinquish his personal capacity to evaluate and reflect and may gradually become unable to exercise this potential without great difficulty.

POINTS FOR CONSIDERATION

Certain possibilities are inherent in this approach. The leader should consider these: (1) the member may receive little benefit due in part to his minimal involvement; (2) the member may not develop sufficient independence and initiative to handle the situations within and without the group; (3) the degree of permissiveness possible in this structure may not accomplish the purpose hoped for by the leader.

The leader's reasonable success could have the following results: (1) members have more information upon which to base decisions; (2) members may make superficial changes in return for positive reinforcement from the leader; (3) members may also accept the suggestions and ideas of the leader and later carefully consider them, deciding to develop new directions; (4) members may become more dependent upon the leader and less interested in developing the ability to solve their problems independently.

The Democratic Group

PURPOSES AND GOALS

The purpose of the democratic group[2] is the development of the potentiality of the individual to work on his own needs and to become able to help others to work on their needs. This is attempted by focusing upon the growth of the whole person. Each member is helped to locate his needs, conceptualize and understand them and to direct his energy intelligently toward a higher quality of behavior. It is assumed that despite the effect of external conditions and influences, the origin and control of each member's behavior is from within himself. Another purpose is to assist each member to respect his recognition of needs and his ability to work toward their satisfaction. The leader works for the improvement of the abilities of members to learn from one another through listening and interaction.

The goal is to assist each member to better understand himself, other members and the process in which he is involved. It is hoped that he will become more mature and responsible in his relationships and more able to use the environment to work toward socially constructive outcomes.

PROCESS

The process is open and developmental. All aspects of member and leader relationships are matters of common concern, and experiences are handled cooperatively. The members and leader explore together the areas of concern to locate the foci of interests, to decide the direction and plan of work, and to determine how they will perform responsibly.

As a member of the group the leader has the same rights

and privileges as others have. He does not abdicate, nor does he dominate. Instead he makes the quality of his experience available. The members accept him as they do one another for his intrinsic contribution to their mutuality.

The quality of the process improves with intelligent practice. Its improvement depends upon the quality of the leader's performance, ongoing evaluation and development of the members' skills. The interaction in the process is three-way, members to one another, members to leader and leader to members. This interaction process develops through experiencing the freedom of expression and a mutual respect for one another's ideas. Indications that the process is improving are greater member satisfaction, an indication of better need fulfilment; a higher operational unity; and the more adequate interpersonal behavior of each member.

Evaluation of the process in each discussion is a necessary and integral part in the development of the group. This is done through the comments of the member who is the leader of the discussion, the remarks of the observer and the cooperative discussion of all. The process is examined at various levels. The actions and reactions of members are clarified and possibilities for improvement are considered. This is a cooperative analysis and resetting of goals in which the leader participates with the group members.

LEADERSHIP

Since many would-be-democratic leaders have been conditioned in authoritarian experiences, the aspiring leader wisely begins by recognizing their influence on him. He should also recognize that democratic procedures may seem to some unrealistic and may be met with opposition, since the culture is oriented toward a competitive way of life. All of these conditions suggest that the democratic leadership of a group is more than learning skills. Essentially it is becoming a democratic person.

In his becoming the leader moves away from the satisfaction of his needs through controlling, directing, informing, analyzing or making suggestions. Increasingly he takes pleasure from indications of improvement of thought, skills and behavior of the members.

Such a leader assumes that the group members are capable and interested in quality interaction. He helps them to clarify their interests and goals and assists them in selecting a topic or problem of mutual concern. He strives to develop and respect their evaluative abilities. The controls and direction are those cooperatively developed and accepted. Together they visualize alternatives, project themselves into ensuing situations and make decisions.

He encourages this improvement through listening, questioning, reacting, and by clarification, reflection and synthesis. In this manner he helps the members to develop situational thinking, assuming that free, thoughtful reflection and interaction produce quality insights and decisions.

The leader provides opportunity for the members to make all the decisions for which they can demonstrate responsibility. This is, of course, within a framework set up by the leader and modified with his own ability to extend freedom to the members and the "unfixed ends" in the particular situation.

Those who succeed in becoming democratic leaders facilitate an environment in which is nurtured a sense of responsibility and caring for one another. This kind of leader encourages freedom of expression, respects each individual as a person and concentrates upon trying to understand the individual and the meaning of his verbal and nonverbal expressions. He is a resource person who extends leadership and planning to the members and thus contributes to their development.

MEMBERSHIP

Each member is seen as a potential contributor and is encouraged to participate by the absence of evaluative comments. Members become willing to consider other points of view, to discuss them freely and to alter or modify their own thinking accordingly. They increase in their understanding and willingness to arrive at conclusions through a consensus. The accepting group atmosphere encourages and facilitates creative differences of expression.

The discussion is generally led by one of the members who has volunteered in advance. All feel responsible to bring ideas to the discussion and to increase their ability to do so. They learn to express these ideas and to use fewer words as they become aware of the importance of sharing time as a part of the helping relationship.

The leader is gradually accepted as a member, though in a different sense. He also expresses ideas which, like those of the other members, are presented only in relation to the particular facet of the topic currently under consideration and with which the members feel free to agree or disagree.

PATTERNS OF USE

The democratic method is used in classrooms, industry, recreation, business, churches and clinics. There is, however, wide variation in the degree of cooperative planning and decision-making which is encouraged. This is the result of one or more of the following conditions: (1) When leaders become threatened and insecure regarding the process or perceived outcomes they are inclined to move toward the authoritarian end of the continuum. (2) Confusion exists, since democratic functioning is sometimes perceived to result completely from the development of skills rather than also through becoming a democratic person. (3) Much "becoming" is necessary before an authoritarian leader can be genuinely democratic.

The exploration of what truly democratic groups can accomplish is hindered by the assumption that groups have proceeded democratically when actually they are a hybrid of authoritarian and democratic attitudes and procedures.

THEORETICAL BASIS

Democratic group process is based on the field theory of learning. Each member is the center of his own field and the emphasis is upon relations between persons. The leader takes an internal self-approach to behavior. That is, he tries to understand the member's behavior from the member's frame of reference. He considers the member's behavior to be a function of his individual perception of the meaning of the situation at the time of response.

Each member understands others better through free and open interaction. Experiences are clarified and individual thought patterns improved. The unit of learning experience is primarily the member facing his own situation, growing out of his needs as he perceives them. His progress is assisted by the emerging intelligence of the members operating as an organic group in areas of their needs.

Each member's meanings and values are accepted as useful to the group. Feelings, thoughts and responses of each are data for intelligent consideration. Through interpersonal relations in the group each member creates new meanings. He increases the quality of his differentiation as he progresses. By these means he improves his understanding of the world, others and himself.

As a result of interaction of group members open to

change, the field (the individual, others and the environment) is a fluid whole always emerging or becoming. Insights and goal-setting are the outcomes of qualitative interaction.

The members gradually become a group. Their integrative unity is characterized by a feeling of safety, acceptance and a sense of responsibility to help one another and the group as a whole. There is a high level of trust of each in the others with reference to individual attitudes and performance.

POINTS FOR CONSIDERATION

It is not easy for an individual conditioned in authoritarianism to become a democratic person. He may experience difficulty with the following: (1) believing that group members are capable of and interested in critical thinking concerning their problems; (2) recognizing "unfixed ends" and using them for growth purposes; (3) developing the members' abilities to evaluate and accept their conclusions; (4) encouraging member interaction, essential to cooperative planning; (5) developing situational thinking as a prerequisite to democratic planning; (6) assisting members to change their stereotypic concept of the leader's role.

The Group-Centered Group[3]

PURPOSES AND GOALS

The release of the group's potential capacities and the development of the members' independence and self-responsibility are the foci of emphasis. These are promoted by the leader, who assists the group in working out its own adjustment and in assuming its responsibility for outcomes.

The goals are determined by the members. The more successful groups develop these conditions: (1) a nonthreatening climate and genuine acceptance; (2) a decrease in barriers to free communication within the individual member and among all the members; and (3) an increase in participation. The leader's genuine caring and his belief in the values and capacities of the members facilitate the development of these conditions.

Reasonable expectations of accomplishment include: (1) understanding of self and of the group-centered process; (2) a degree of sensitivity to the feelings and needs of others; (3) self-reliance and responsibility to oneself and others; (4) the ability to use communication skills; and (5) skill in critical thinking.

PROCESS

This process is a new experience for many. Each member experiences a different kind of understanding and learns what it means to give and receive emotional support. Those who have an incorrect picture of themselves come to see and accept themselves as they really are.

In this group climate, each member rebuilds his own value system with a minimal imposition of the value system of the leader. In fact, the leader is careful to support the right of each member to determine his own way of life. The member not only gives help but receives it as well. The experience assists each to achieve a balance between independence and realistic dependence and to feel a responsibility toward others.

The leader initiates the members into a permissive, accepting situation in which they assume direction for the goals and the process. He does this by indicating that the group can develop and follow its own leads. Some groups are able to get started almost immediately but many have considerable difficulty.

The process proceeds through themes. A theme is a topic or emphasis which disappears and reappears. It may reappear several times with added and deeper meaning. The general movement of the themes which do reappear is toward greater detail and deeper emotional response.

The process has both positive and negative elements. The positive elements are expressed in insights, plans and attitudes toward self and others. Negative elements are expressed in the form of nonparticipation, defensive remarks, and attitudes toward self and others. Generally, negative elements increase gradually until they reach a climax and then decrease, but positive elements increase within the session and within the whole experience.

The process resembles daily living in that there are problems remaining at the end of each session and at the end of the total experience. Thus it blends naturally into daily life.

Members vary in the degree to which they benefit from the experience. Those who benefit most are apparently more able and more interested in focusing on their own and others' problems of living and become more responsible in helping the other members in their understanding of them. Those who benefit least focus more on intellectual problems and are more prodding in their interaction with other members. They avoid focusing on their own perceptions and feelings.

An important aspect of the process is the possibility of releasing the therapeutic potential of the group itself. As the number of sessions increases, some members both verbally and nonverbally facilitate the conditions which help others to gain insight and to feel supported in their efforts toward gaining self-understanding and understanding of others.

LEADERSHIP

Group-centered leadership is difficult to attain. To a large degree this is because the leader must be able to believe in the capacity of the group member to select an alternative, to plan a method of progress, and to evaluate outcomes. The leader finds it most difficult to believe and accept the following: (1) that the group members are able to evaluate and will do so; (2) that their evaluations will advance the progress of the group; and (3) that in doing so they will increase their intelligence regarding interpersonal relationships.

The leader's interest in each member is conveyed through his genuine warmth and empathy and his nonevaluative attitude. He listens in order to understand the meaning of each member's contribution. He clarifies, reflects meanings, links members' ideas, synthesizes, and summarizes. He receives satisfactions from indications that the members are developing their potential capacities, becoming more interdependent and adequate, and increasing their sense of responsibility. He attains these outcomes by endeavoring to facilitate the following: (1) free communication within and among all members of the group; (2) a nonthreatening, accepting psychological climate; (3) an increasing opportunity for participation.

The group-centered leader holds different beliefs about the members and the process than do leaders of other groups. He differs in his attitude toward people. Through his interaction he conveys the confidence he has in the group members and in their ability and willingness to be responsible for themselves.

The leader develops his skill in spacing, timing, and frequency of participation. Skills and insights develop slowly. The leader is a participating member but his purpose is to facilitate interaction and insight, not to intrude, direct, or dominate. This is especially important in the early development of the group.

MEMBERSHIP

The kind of listening which members develop in an evaluative, competitive environment is an impediment to understanding. In the group-centered process they gradually learn to listen from a nonevaluative framework.

They come to know the true meaning of acceptance as they experience listening and being listened to regardless of the nature or length of contribution. As caring and respect develop, they are able to be what they really are. They discover that differences in values, attitudes, and expressions can add a perspective to their understanding. Silent periods become acceptable and more comfortable.

Members gradually become more able to respond to one another and to use the skills of clarification, reflection, and summarization as they become necessary. Each member assumes some of the leadership functions. In this way distributive leadership emerges and becomes a natural pattern. The members improve greatly in their use of time and in their ability to focus on various aspects of a problem. They grow in spontaneity and experience a sense of adequacy.

PATTERNS OF USE

Group-centered principles have proved useful in all forms of education, management, counseling and therapy. At present their use is limited only by the leader's conviction and faith in applying them to interpersonal relationships. A leader who would become a group-centered leader requires time to develop because in-depth personality change in himself is a prerequisite. It is not surprising, then, that there are pseudo-group-centered groups just as there are pseudo-democratic groups.

THEORETICAL BASIS

The theoretical basis of group functioning is self-theory. Self-theory makes several assumptions about personality and personality change. Its basic assumption is that the self has a single goal—that of realizing itself in accordance with its nature. This is expressed through a creative biological urge which motivates a continuous striving against most difficult odds. This "rationality of the organism" is considered dependable and is oriented toward constructive development. The development is through differentiation and expansion, and the individual becomes progressively more capable in decision-making and more autonomous.

This increasingly constructive development is an outcome of the individual's perception, knowledge and symbolization (ideas and meanings derived from experience). Added to these is the satisfaction of his ego needs.

Foremost in the member's growth is the nature of his perception. He plans and makes decisions in terms of reactions to the experience of his perceptions. The correctness of his perceptions bears a direct relation to his self-image, his feeling of safety, security and adequacy. Unless he feels insecure, inadequate and threatened, he checks his tentative impressions against other sources of information. His perceptions are conscious and subconscious, and both kinds affect the resulting behavior.

Knowledge enables the member to distinguish between more and less mature ways of behaving. Useful knowledge results from interaction with the leader and other members. Interaction aids understanding, furthers appreciation and develops values. Some values may be "taken over" from others and changed in the process. It is hoped that uncritical acceptance of another's values will take place less frequently in an accepting, nonthreatening atmosphere. It is assumed that the member will make a constructive choice if he can really consider various possibilities without being "swayed" by others' opinions. It is further assumed that it is possible for the member to know himself better than someone else is able to know him, even with the utilization of the best methods and instruments.

How much a member reflects upon the group experience influences his development as a member. Members vary greatly in their ability to evaluate experience without being warped by the ideas of significant other people. How well experiences can be considered and assimilated depends on how much threat the member is experiencing. Threatening ideas need to be examined in an accepting and safe psychological relationship if they are to be considered without distortion. Recognizing this, the leader is constantly alert to reduce threat and thus increase the possibility of the member's consideration of ideas and feelings necessary to his development.

All members have ego needs. One set of needs arises from the desire to be accepted and respected by others. Those who have a great need to be well-liked may conclude that this is possible only in relation to one's appearance, behavior, quality of work or degree of conformity. A second set of needs derives from the desire to be useful, to be of service, to help a cause or a friend, or to be involved in a constructive undertaking. A person may be respected by others and yet remain dissatisfied because his need to be useful is not met. Introspection becomes an instrument for assessing one's relation to this need satisfaction.

Further assumptions focus on the conditions of change, therapy and growth. It is assumed that the safe, genuine climate in which the leader completely accepts the member facilitates change and growth. In this climate it is assumed that the member will perceive, focus and examine experiences formerly never accepted as being part of him. Or if he did recognize that they were part of the way he is, he concluded that they were so infrequent that they were not really representative of him. In this climate of acceptance and safety, he is able to accept himself as he really is—both what is excellent about him and what is not. The rate at which this process moves is slow, but it is assumed that once he begins, he will continue with steady persistence.

POINTS FOR CONSIDERATION

This group differs significantly from other groups in both theory and practice. Members become increasingly group-centered persons. Competitive and evaluative attitudes are replaced by understanding and acceptance only through time and much effort.

Many have been so conditioned in authoritarian patterns that they feel insecure in others. Members generally have looked to the leader for direction and stimulation and they have a stereotype image of what the leader should be and do. Therefore both his acceptance of them as persons and the method he uses are confusing and, for some, disturbing in the beginning. When they come to understand him, his ideas receive the same consideration as those of other members.

Increasing member participation develops within the accepting climate. It cannot be verbally encouraged or forced. There is a marked improvement in listening and concentration as the group develops. There is also a growing understanding of the process and progress in its evaluation. Spontaneity develops with expression of both ideas and feelings. A growing sense of responsibility for the welfare of others and the progress of the group steadily increases.

The T Group[4]

This group is basically different from the group-centered group although at first glance it appears to be similar in many respects. It is different in its assumptions regarding what induces change in behavior and in the method used by the leader, who is called a trainer. It is similar in its dependence upon the responsible and caring relationship of each member for all other members. This is the relationship considered necessary for genuine change to take place. It is also similar to the group-centered group in the emphasis which is placed on the development of skills. Leaders in both groups facilitate permissiveness and acceptance, but in the T group these are restricted to the purposes of the setting as viewed by the leader. In the group-centered group, permissiveness and acceptance are unconditional.

PURPOSES AND GOALS

The T-group method may have education, counseling or therapy for its chief purpose. Although all groups may resemble one another in various ways, the orientations are different:

In general, T groups have three goals: (1) the development of behavioral skills; (2) the development of the ability to perceive the consequences of one's actions and to learn from this; and (3) the development of concepts and theoretical insights which aid in understanding group functioning and its relation to personal goals and values.

Theoretical concepts are presented through lectures. Trainers agree that information is necessary but disagree regarding the substance, frequency, and method of presentation. Generally three kinds of theoretical materials are presented: (1) community and role dynamics; (2) behavioral change, change agents, and application; and (3) individual and small-group dynamics. Some trainers fear that an over-emphasis on content may cause the members to intellectualize and avoid the emotional problems.

Enthusiasts view the T group as exceptionally useful in inducing the kind and degree of involvement deemed necessary for individual change to take place.

PROCESS

The process is designed to overcome the passivity which many consider a handicap in formal learning, or, in other words, to involve members immediately at a depth perceived as necessary for internal resistances to be overcome and value orientations to be challenged.

There are three general emphases: (1) values and information; (2) the use of ambiguity and frustration to secure optimal involvement; and (3) the intervention of the trainer, which is focused on the "here and now" of what is taking place in the group.

These emphases are put into effect in the following manner: (1) Structure is minimal. Outlines, description of procedures, planned methods and requirements are not provided. This results in ambiguity and frustration. Motivation is assumed to result from the incongruity between the members' expectancies and the actual group experiences. (2) The trainer intervenes. Most trainers are not members of the group. They intervene in order to help the members examine what is taking place in the group. Their interventions may be in the form of questions, interpretations, suggestions or advice. For example, a trainer may direct attention to the fact that much time is being spent on discussing situations outside the group (the "there and then"), and very little on the current ("here and now") problems of the members, indicating that apparently they are not ready to discuss present happenings in the group. (3) The immediate experiences of the group are considered the basic ingredients of learning and the focus of emphasis. (4) Members are challenged to develop the skills of inquiry and evaluation, reassess the adequacy of their value orientations and social perspectives, accept the responsibility for reducing internal barriers, and develop the ability not only to give help but to receive it from others. (5) Members are assisted in self-study. Several means are used, such as pre- and post-rating scales; lectures delivered to the entire enrollment (which may be several groups); members listening to taped sessions; and the use of groups of two members, each interviewing the other in turn.

Learning results from the interaction of each member with other members. He develops the ability to take the initiative in both giving and receiving. In this development, he achieves to some degree a self-identity which is active and reflective, and engages in realistic relationships.

The focus of learning has two dimensions. First, the method is planned to encourage each member to test the reality and depth of his conscious dissatisfactions. The second evolves from the first by providing situations in which the member recognizes and confronts dissatisfactions not previously perceived.

THEORETICAL BASES

The T group is a multiple-theory group. That is, it uses all the principles and methods of the other group patterns—authoritarian, democratic, and group-centered. It is actually an amalgamation of several theories of learning and behavioral change. In the use of the lecture and the interventions of the trainer, it relies upon leader dominance and the association theory of learning. In the encouragement of member-to-member interaction in relation to what the members have chosen to discuss, it relies upon the field theory or the democratic approach. The final stage of the T-group process is marked by more acceptance and permissiveness and there is a movement toward the self-theory of the group-centered group.

Thus there is no consistent theoretical basis. Various theories and methods are used by the same leader if and when he considers them useful. No two T-group experiences are identical or even very similar. Each trainer operates with the group in terms of his psychological needs and his theoretical leanings, emphasizing the method which accords with the theories in which he most strongly believes. Trainers also vary in the degree of emphasis they place on the "here and now" of what is actually taking place in the group as compared with the "there and then" of other situations.

LEADERSHIP

There is great variation in the needs, beliefs and methods of the leaders. Part of this is due to their past educational experiences. Some trainers lean heavily toward action research concepts, others toward organization and mental health concepts, and still others toward the clinical and psychiatric positions. There is considerable variation in the professional background of trainers. This accounts in part for the great dissimilarity in the reports of the experiences of members who have participated in T groups.

Trainers vary in relation to their conclusions concerning the following problems: the direction the group should take toward skill development, behavioral change or therapy; the use of feedback and to what degree it should be used, i.e., the form it will take—role-playing, simulation experiments, or data-gathering instruments such as questionnaires. Other decisions are concerned with how much emphasis to place on the discussion of what is currently taking place in the group; what feelings to work with and at what level; how much reliance to place on the emergent qualities of the group; and how much responsibility to assume for the direction and guidance of these qualities.

There are other considerations in the area of needs and beliefs. Is the trainer interested in understanding himself? To what degree can he be open concerning his motivations, beliefs, attitudes, and feelings? How great is his need to protect himself and the members?

The way in which he answers these questions determines in large measure the character of his trainer performance.

Some trainers remain outside the group. They take no part in the discussion of content and serve the group chiefly as process analysts. They do this by analysis, questions and suggestions. Those trainers who do not participate in topical discussions believe that their participation would determine the content. They assume that members would come to know the topics of most interest to the trainer and would either move the discussions away from or toward these topics.

A small minority of trainers enter the group as members, but these generally conclude that by doing so they greatly decrease the effectiveness of their interventions. The majority of trainers withdraw from the group and thus induce member tensions and frustrations. These feelings in large measure result from the accompanying ambiguity and lack of satisfactory procedural organization. This method is believed to greatly increase member involvement. All trainers attempt, through their performance, to facilitate concern-resolution, group growth, personal growth, and defense reduction.

MEMBER PARTICIPATION

The usual initial reaction to the lack of trainer direction and resultant ambiguity is one of frustration and the display of aggression toward the trainer. Members wonder how they are going to learn unless he does more. They do not perceive trainer intervention as supplying the help which they feel is needed.

This is followed by brief efforts to look at what is taking place in the group. These efforts are interspersed with discussions of general topics.

A sharp cleavage generally develops in the next stage. Some members are bothered, threatened or disturbed by the efforts of other members to understand member interaction and individual member behavior.

On the other hand, some members realize that they must work out ways of relating to one another and of setting standards. These members are not just satisfied to increase interaction. They wish to understand its meaning both for the group and for themselves.

A number of the members are apprehensive and concerned about the interpretation of one another's actions, ideas and feelings. They feel that some of the members may be hurt. That is, their ego strength may not be sufficient to withstand psychological attack and to make use of it. There is some cause for concern, since a small minority do become disturbed and maladjusted and occasionally someone may even suffer a mental breakdown.

Members who are not apprehensive often feel (and rightly so) that they lack the skill to participate. Much depends on the trainer in this crucial period when members are under pressure from others to reveal their goals, ideas and fears. The professional, experienced trainer is generally able to estimate the strength of a member's ego. He recognizes the need to protect the members from moving too fast in self-discovery and in reducing one another's defenses too rapidly.

In a well-conducted group, fears gradually subside and

trust develops. Then members begin to experiment in discussing the current issues in the group. As they sense one another's support, they become better listeners. Cooperative thinking and problem-solving improve. Members report that the progress in this state seems to occur almost unnoticed. They sense the necessity to maintain a balance between meeting individual needs and maintaining continuity in group tasks.

PATTERNS OF USE

For some time, T groups were used increasingly in programs of management development for in-service education. This was done for the purpose of resolving the problems of communication, interpersonal relations, belonging, and loneliness which confront the individual within a bureaucratic organization.

Although management has recognized the need for more human relationships to permit meaningful interpersonal exchange, the T group has been subjected to questioning and doubt. Over a half-dozen of the large national companies no longer encourage employees to enroll in T groups.

One reason for this change in attitude is the difficulty for employees to adjust to work conditions following such training. The methods of the T group *per se* do not transfer well to everyday relationships. People generally are not accustomed to revealing their motives and drives or to having them diagnosed by others.

The T group is also used extensively in preparing professionals in helping occupations. It is also being applied to the socialization process of children, youth and college students.

POINTS FOR CONSIDERATION

The assumptions regarding how people learn in the T group are not new. The theory is authoritarian-association theory with some overlay of pseudo-self-theory. The differences in learning between the traditional authoritarian and T group are the conditions under which learning is considered to take place. These are evident in the emphasis placed upon the examination of interpersonal and intrapersonal events of the process as it takes place. Each member is considered to be a reactive individual. The problem is to induce him to react in such a way that he will become sufficiently involved to learn.

To ensure the degree of involvement deemed necessary the members are introduced to a mildly traumatic situation. The feeling of ambiguity, frustration, and apprehension which is created is assumed to be a necessary prerequisite to learning. This state is relied upon to reduce inhibitions and promote regression considered conducive to exploration of members' psychological conditions. It may be questionable to assume that such an experience is necessary to involve members sufficiently and in depth. Persons who have found normal and useful outlets for their aggressions and hostilities, and are genuinely caring, responsible persons usually do not need such an experience to induce involvement.

The Encounter Group

The term "encounter group" is used to refer to all sensitivity, basic encounter, and awareness groups and other forms of current encounter experiences. There appears to be much diversity among them, but the real differences are not significant.

The encounter group has received widespread popularity. There are several explanations for its acceptance. One is the evolving viewpoint of society regarding how change in behavior takes place. A second explanation is man's existential anxiety which results in large part from the loss of symbols and interest in the symbolic. The trend is away from dependence on analysis and insight toward a dependence upon experience and the assumption that improvement in behavior can and does take place without insight. From this perspective the encounter group is antithetical to the assumptions of Western religions. Third, unlike the leaders in group psychotherapy, many leaders of encounter groups are trained only in the social and behavioral sciences. They may be teachers, ministers, publishers, artists and others imbued with a certain call to help humanity.

The members are chiefly from the middle class. Large numbers are college students, management and supervisory personnel, church-related people and persons from all walks of life who are dissatisfied or lonely. Leaders of encounter groups accept everyone who applies and may even solicit customers. It is assumed that everyone needs encounter and is capable of engaging in it. On the one hand, many persons live creative and useful lives without experiencing an encounter group. On the other hand, it is in large measure because people cannot encounter that they come to these groups. Many of them are depressed and feel that their lives are empty.

PURPOSES AND GOALS

This type of group experience is intensive. Its purpose is to facilitate a high degree of member involvement. Through dynamic open interaction it is expected that each member will achieve deeper understanding of himself and his relationship to others; that he will change his personal attitudes and behavior, and that as a result he will be able to relate more effectively to others in his everyday life situation.

The benefits take many forms, such as fulfillment, realization, awareness, efficiency, joy, peace, unity and love. The tenets of the process are being offered as a new method of general education. The method emphasizes the emotional rather than the cognitive and poses as freedom's approach to growth.

PROCESS

Burton[5] describes the process as a response of the whole person. It is an "acting out" rather than mere "wishing"; its emphasis falls on the external rather than internal. One puts aside one's reputation, or throws discretion to the winds. Encounter in this setting often makes it possible to release repression immediately in a burst of affection or aggression, without having to accept the usual consequences of these acts. Rogers[6] views it as a varied tapestry, but within any one group he discerns certain patterns. Tentatively, he lists these patterns (based upon tape recordings and personal reports): (1) milling around, (2) resistance to personal expression or exploration, (3) description of past feelings, (4) expression of negative feelings, (5) expression and exploration of personally meaningful material, (6) expression of immediate interpersonal feelings in the group, (7) the development of a healing capacity in the group, (8) self-acceptance and the beginning of change, (9) the cracking of façades, (10) feedback to the individual, (11) confrontation, (12) the helping relationship outside the group session, (13) the basic encounter.

The process is complex and varies to some degree with different groups in relation to the openness of the members and their ability to tolerate ambiguity. It also varies greatly with the leadership. There are almost as many kinds of groups as there are leaders. They vary in relation to the psychological needs of the leader, the degree to which he himself is open; his belief regarding how change in behavior takes place; his respect for the capacity of the members; and his ability to trust them to progress in their relationships.

The process is relatively unstructured. The experiences—especially the initial ones—are planned to provide ambiguity, uncertainty, and lack of leadership direction as a means of increasing involvement of the members. Direct confrontation of one member with another is central to the process.

The members choose the goals and each decides his own personal direction. Each member becomes aware of the fact that he will experience considerable pressure from the other members to "tell it like it is." It is expected that the members will move through confusion, uncertainty, frustration, fractionation and discontinuity to a climate of coherence, trust, and some feeling of mutual responsibility.

LEADERSHIP

The leader perceives himself to be a facilitator of some thought but chiefly of feeling. He performs from within the group but not as a member of the group. In the initial stages he is especially permissive, but he is also interpretative and evaluative. He uses questions as he thinks necessary to encourage deeper exploration of the problem by the one presenting it. At times the dialogue is between one member and other members. Other members are interpretative and evaluative. At times they even demand that the member continue the exploration of his feelings.

Leaders of encounter groups use several methods in relation to their perception of the current need. The fact that they are often theoretically inconsistent appears to be of little concern. The degree to which the leader is authoritative and analytical depends upon his personality needs and his beliefs regarding what is necessary to achieve a useful therapeutic experience. Those leaders who are more democratic or client-centered personalities would be expected to conduct the group differently from those who are benevolent authoritarians at heart.

MEMBERSHIP

Members in general are frustrated to some degree by the lack of structure and goals. This situation is counted on to involve the members actively and to eliminate the usual passivity. A lack of involvement is assumed to exist if the leader provides security through structure and the setting of goals. A high degree of involvement is the expected outcome of the ambiguous and changing environment.

Such an environment affects the members in various ways and usually forces each into some kind of confrontation with the others. The situation gradually generates the expression of negative feelings toward one another, the leader, and the purposes of the group. In this way the leader feels he has set the stage for genuine exploration of personal and interpersonal feelings and the development of insights leading to personality change. After the members have attacked one another, breaking down the protective defenses, they gradually change in their attitudes from the negative and critical to the constructive and helpful.

The members gradually move from talking of the past or situations outside the group to dialogue concerned with what is taking place within the group. This is frequently referred to as a movement from a discussion of the "there and then" situations to the "here and now" situations.

The evolution of this process increases the pressure on each member to open himself up to the group, not only to gain self-insight but also to remain a respectable and respected member. Those members who have revealed themselves are not in a mood to permit a more sensitive, more inhibited or more threatened member to progress at his own rate.

After a member has begun to discuss his fears, anxieties

and concerns, he is not permitted to stop, or hesitate or even proceed as he wishes. The leader or members question, probe and "push" to get the completed story or to cause him to come to grips with the situation. He probably concludes by "telling all," but it does not necessarily follow that this is what he really wished to do. Uncertainties remain. Has the split within him been overcome? Will the "healing" of the members who pressured him to reveal himself be able to restore him to himself? Unless he now has a worthy dedication, he could end up like the man in the New Testament story who rid his house of an evil spirit, only to find that seven others came in and took up their abode.

PATTERNS OF USE

As indicated earlier, the encounter group has many labels. The actual form varies widely in relation to the needs and beliefs of the leaders. The groups also vary with reference to purpose and duration. Some are continuous over a period of many hours or over a weekend with time only for rest. These encourage an intensity and endurance which sets them apart and are generally known as marathon groups.

The chief commonality is that all forms are planned to facilitate an encounter between persons in a group environment. Purposes of groups vary from the educational one of learning skills in human relations to the therapeutic one of self-understanding and understanding of others. This is especially true in relation to maladjustive patterns of behavior.

THEORETICAL BASES

Many theories, contradictory in their assumptions, form the bases of the encounter experience. This condition is the result of wide experimentation in an attempt to develop helpful procedures. Attention to theoretical considerations came later. Among the mixture of the theoretical entanglements the most common theories are Lewinian and client-centered. These are heavily overlaid with Gestalt theory and various brands of psychoanalytic theory. That is, the theoretical assumptions vary from permissiveness and acceptance to the opposite—control, direction and unacceptance. They also vary from looking for behavioral causes within a context which gives them meaning to looking at change as an event resulting from a previous event in an ongoing chain of events.

The theoretical assumptions of the leader determine which theories receive greater emphases. The multiple theoretical bases of operation are only as multiple as the leader is. For most leaders the chief base is authoritarian and analytical with some simulated overtones of self-theory.

Members soon recognize that acceptance and permissiveness are limited and conditional. These conditions prevail only to the degree that the results conform to the leader's plans and ideas.

The leader is chiefly interested in furthering a high degree of involvement. He is not concerned with the means he uses to induce it. He is not interested in being consistent. He does what he believes will get results. He rules against passivity but uses lectures to impart ideas, although listening to a lecture is a relatively passive experience. In this and other ways leaders maintain an implicit belief in association learning which is in conflict with their emphasis on field theory, i.e., starting with the problems of members within the "field" or group environment.

POINTS FOR CONSIDERATION

The leader attempts to increase the members' involvement with one another at some depth and within a limited space of time. He insists on reaction to one another in relation to the "here and now" of the group experience. No one is to avoid interaction or refuse it.

He expects that the group will move through these stages: descriptive personal comments with emphasis on past experience, beginning reactions to one another concerning the ongoing comments, explosive interactions of a negative and/or aggressive nature, the "pressure cooker" stage in which each reveals himself to all the others, and the reconciling and positive interactions, sometimes referred to as "the love feast."

There are several matters concerning the process which need consideration. Negative action has become the initial expectancy of the leader. He may create this expectancy in the group and the member may engage in negativism, since this is what he has come to believe is expected.

The assumption that everyone needs this kind of process and will benefit from it should be re-examined. There has been little follow-up on this process and therefore no solid basis for knowing its dangers or usefulness with any degree of certainty. Rogers made a follow-up study of 400 participants. About 2 per cent of those involved felt it had been "damaging" or "more unhelpful than helpful." About 6 per cent saw it as "mostly frustrating, annoying or confusing." About 33 per cent saw it as "constructive in its results"; and 50 per cent, as a "deeply meaningful positive experience." The remainder were neutral. William Schutz reports that about 80 per cent of the participants in encounter groups found them helpful. But will those who have a genuine personal center, a sincere respect for themselves and constructive expectancies concerning others benefit from this kind of process? May they find it unnecessary to become emotionally, defensively and aggressively involved? Could it be that interpretations which others make of them have only minor effect, and that those which they perceive as having some merit may be accepted and not call forth a defensive reaction?

It could be that they already possess ego strength and self-respect, and they reflect upon it and measure its validity quietly and unobtrusively. Some people are capable of this. Such persons do not need such an experience and are not helped by reacting in a hasty, impulsive, unexamined, irresponsible and emotional manner.

There may be some reason to doubt that the final phase of the encounter group is one of responsible caring. The members are under pressure to cooperate and help one another, and their behavior may be only a simulation of caring and love. Under such conditions many may respond to the situation by asking: What should I do? What am I to do? What can I get out of it? Such persons are not engaged in the creative risk of genuine love. Although many are helped in encounter groups, many questions remain about the methods.

The Participation-Training Group

PURPOSE

The purpose of this group[7] is to train members and leaders to perform more efficiently in adult education groups. The authors carefully differentiate between this form of discussion group and the "usual discussion group." A few of the major differences are the following: The discussion group has no definite means of improving its function. It is content-centered and its main objective is the learning of subject matter. The topics (content) are chosen by the leader and often centered on "issues found in resource materials or defined by the resource person."

On the other hand, the participation-training group has a trainer whose function is to help the group realize effective participation through brief lectures and by his interventions in the discussions. Also each session ends with an open appraisal. The members always choose the topic by consensus. The chief objective of participation training is to learn to share in leadership by being a responsible group member and to understand oneself and others as learners.

PROCESS

In some minor respects it resembles a T group. It operates with a trainer who uses the same methods of intervention with questions, suggestions and directions. Similarly, it also focuses on the "here and now" of the process in the group. The trainer in participation training uses brief lectures focused only on the process. In the T group, the trainer lectures on such topics as "community" and "role dynamics" and "behavioral change." Trainers of both groups remain apart from the members.

The discussion in participation training is led by a participant who volunteers to lead for one or two sessions. The trainer does not contribute to the discussion. His function is to improve the functioning of the leader and the participants. The trainer hopes to improve the process by interrupting the discussion at crucial times in order to help the group analyze its process and procedures.

THEORETICAL ASSUMPTIONS

Participation training relies on contrasting theoretical assumptions. There is permissiveness and acceptance with reference to the members' choice of topics. In the conduct of the group, the leader uses a quasi-authoritarian method, guiding the group in relation to a preplanned outline. The trainer is authoritarian and analytical in his training method. That is, he interrupts, analyzes, interprets, suggests, lectures and questions.

Emphasis is placed on the fact that the trainer has no treatment function. He assumes the difficult task of emphasizing sociodynamics and avoiding psychodynamics. That is, he concentrates on the current relationships between participants and not on the workings of individual personalities. It is questionable if a true distinction can be made within such an artificial setting.

Such training does little more than improve one's discussion skills. Even in this area, the skills improved upon are derived from authoritarian assumptions regarding leadership functions. As such they have the inherent weaknesses of authoritarian methods.

No assumption is made that the members will become more sensitive to one another's feelings or develop the desire and ability to assume any responsibility for helping one another toward greater personal maturity. Mutual caring, the essence of a true group, is not anticipated and no provision is made for its encouragement. The symbolic interpersonal relationships of love, caring, responsibility and openness are not assumed to have an integral part, nor are they mentioned as being desirable to the learner in his efforts. Even learning itself is considered to be chiefly or only an intellectual venture. Self-understanding is not encouraged for the purpose of understanding oneself but for the purpose of understanding how one learns. Thus there is a false dichotomy which sets up learning as an activity apart from one's feelings and attitudes. This is an unfortunate assumption, since it is well established that emotion is an integral part of all human functioning. Not only this, but if genuine change is one of the hoped-for outcomes, then the total involvement of the learner on the feeling, acting and thinking levels is required. On the other hand, genuine change is not posited as a goal of the activity. This is another way in which participation training is not a true group method.

POINTS FOR CONSIDERATION

Those planning to use participation training (often known as the Indiana Plan) should be sure that their hoped-for outcomes are in accordance with the aims of the training. In addition to this, they should become conversant with the clearly written manual *Participation Training for Adult Education* (see Author's Notes: Chap. 3, No. 7) in order to determine whether or not they would desire to function as a trainer and if they believe the method is in keeping with what they desire group process to accomplish in their organization.

4 *GROUP PROCESS*

What Is Group Process?[1]

MEANING OF PROCESS

The word *process* indicates the dynamic nature of a group. In its broadest sense, process is so completely coexistent with life that when it ceases, life ceases. Process in any organism is a continuous, dynamic and directional movement. This includes all that takes place within the individual and his relationships with his external environment.

In other words, process is the sum total of a person's experience. Part of this takes place when he is alone and part when he is in relation with others. The experience he has when alone we term individual process and when with others, group process. Group process may be described as two or more persons working together on a need or problem toward some recognized end. They use some form of interpersonal relations with some effect on each.

But not all groups of two or more people are the same. In some groups the interaction is from one person to another. There is no attempt at wholeness or at any deepening of interpersonal relationships. This form of group interaction is often referred to as social group behavior.

THREE-WAY PROCESS

At first sight, various groups may resemble the three-way-process group, but there are some significant qualitative differences. In the latter group there is a tangible qualitative interdependence of each member upon the others which operates in three ways: member to member, member to the whole, and the whole to the member. When this three-dimensional relationship breaks down, we have only social behavior, or in some instances, the process of an authoritarian group. The group process of the true or organic group requires this three-dimensional relationship.

This three-way-process relationship is necessary in order to release an emergent quality of cooperative unity. It is through this psychological climate and this kind of interaction that each member discovers and develops his inner capacities, realizes better the nature of his self, releases more of his past experiences, and learns how to create this emergent quality in all life situations.

The development of this quality of group process demands of its members a high degree of interpersonal responsiveness based on caring and a sense of responsibility. To be most useful to the group, each member must realize that he is accepted regardless of what he produces.

POSSIBILITIES FOR SELF-RENEWAL

The permissive and accepting conditions possible in group process and the motivation accruing from group interaction have especially beneficial results. Many of the members' resistances disappear, facilitating the verbalization of anxiety, guilt, and intrapersonal and interpersonal conflicts. Some of these find direct expression in the group, and others find acceptable outlets through sublimation. Also the member's concept of himself is enhanced through the sense of belonging, support and protection. Painful feelings of inadequacy, stigma and isolation are relieved through the recognition that others have similar problems and that all are experiencing the same things.

A real-life situation becomes possible for an individual in the presence of a number of others like himself, each with his needs and behavior patterns. This supplies the member with many opportunities for acting out his own attitudes and activities as a part of group experience. It also increases his awareness of his own functioning, while the reactions of the members and/or leader give him added insight into his motivations.

Although each of us receives much help in talking with individuals in a one-to-one relationship, the group process has further possibilities. These possibilities which are not included in the individual relationship include: (1) the acceptance of a group of persons with whom the person may test his evolving attitudes and ideas; (2) the motivation which results from acceptance and from experiencing one's own changing attitudes; (3) communication with others which improves the possibility of one's developing genuine interpersonal relationships; (4) the encouragement which stems from the participation of others in trying to solve their conflicts; (5) the sense of safety and belonging which results from the acceptance and understanding of peers and which supports the process of introspection and expression of feeling in depth.

These beneficial outcomes are provided only in the group process that has certain characteristics. Basic is the three-way interaction of the members and leader. Other requisites are a willingness of the members to involve themselves and to modify their attitudes, an unconditional acceptance felt by each member in relation to all the others, and a sense of responsibility and caring for one another's welfare and for the maintenance of the group.

Listening

One of the basic ingredients of group process is listening.[2] Unfortunately, it is assumed that listening develops in the course of communication. However, listening is so important that its development should not be left to chance. To become a good listener requires persistent effort over a long period of time.

KINDS OF LISTENING

The kind of listening we do bears a direct relationship to our purposes for doing so. The most common purposes for listening vary from evaluation to discerning omissions, illogical statements or lack of information. In this framework we listen in order to be able to present our own ideas, suggestions and alternatives more effectively. Most of us have been conditioned to listen in this fashion. We listen to hear what is said, its meaning and its quality in relation to our way of thinking.

There is another way of listening which is much less common. This is listening for the purpose of trying to help another to understand himself and the interaction. Each listens to understand the speaker's meaning and how he feels about what he is saying. This is listening to see the world from the other's point of view as far as possible.

The listening of both members and leaders varies along a continuum from listening in the evaluative sense to listening in the acceptance sense. However, most of the time the listening of the leaders of authoritarian groups, T groups, basic encounter groups and sensitivity groups corresponds with that of the first kind described. That is, those people listen within an evaluative framework. The listening of leaders in democratic groups and especially in group-centered groups corresponds with that of the second description most of the time. That is, they listen within a framework of acceptance.

LISTENING AND BEHAVIORAL CHANGE

In each instance leaders listen as they do because of the nature of their belief concerning behavioral change.

Leaders of authoritarian, basic encounter, sensitivity, and T groups believe that change is chiefly the result of insight gained through the use of critical thought. Thus their evaluations, interpretations, advice and suggestions are considered a means to that end. These leaders who listen evaluatively believe that change will gradually take place in members who can be helped to recognize their present behavior and to some degree understand it. Such listening is similar to that to which the members are accustomed. The difference is that leaders who are chiefly evaluative in their listening become more skilled and more aware of the effects of their responses on the members.

Leaders of the second type, who listen within a framework of acceptance, have a different belief regarding behavioral change. They believe that a climate of acceptance and understanding makes it possible for members to change. The leader's listening flows from the assumption that the group member needs to improve communication within himself. This is considered to lead to better interpersonal relations.

This kind of listening makes unique demands on the leader and poses some threat. The chief demand is the necessity that the leader be able to accept the members as persons regardless of their behaviors and ideas. Such unconditional acceptance is a developmental process, the result in part of the leader's dedication to the ideal.

The threat is present because of the risk involved. To understand another from his viewpoint means identifying with that person to a significant degree. Since the leader suspends judgment and withholds evaluation, he runs the risk of having his view being altered or possibly adopted by another. For the leader to enter into this kind of relationship requires a good measure of personal security and courage, knowing that he himself may be changed in the process.

EFFECTS OF LISTENING

Listening within the framework of either evaluation or acceptance has far-reaching effects which deepen as the number of sessions increases. In the evaluative framework, the members adopt the leader's method of listening and the manner of his responses. Threat is heightened and confrontations among members increase. A forced openness, it is hoped, will lead to members' acceptance of one another. This is considered the prerequisite for coming together in understanding. It is assumed that the expression of negative and conflictual feelings precedes self-understanding of others. In the final stage members frequently come to respect and care for one another with the development of some sense of responsibility.

In the second instance of listening with acceptance, members develop a new feeling of adequacy. This results from the experience of being listened to and understood. When members do not experience devaluation, there is a helpful reduction of threat. Reduction of threat initiates the possibility that members will drop their defensiveness. A lowering of defense leads to more flexible thinking and better problem-solving, and this prepares the way for new understandings.

When a member is heard with interest and understanding by other members and the leader, he makes an effort to express his feelings, ideas and opinions clearly. Group members, observing that the leader is listening with understanding, begin to listen to one another with increasing attention and a growing desire to understand.

As genuineness and interest in understanding develop, members can expect, accept and encourage in one another the expression of their creative differences. They do this in relation to the "there and then" and later the "here and now" of the members' thoughts and feelings.

CONCLUSIONS

We listen as we do because of the kinds of persons we are. The members and leaders who feel adequate and secure hear more and with less distortion than those who are threatened and fearful. Also those who are congruent, who listen because they are interested in helping one another and the process, exert a much more beneficial influence than those who listen because they feel that they should. In most situations improvement in interpersonal relationships necessitates improvement in listening. Good group process requires good listening.

Developing Necessary Skills

Many skills are involved in group process which are necessary to the optimal functioning of the group. Although these skills are integrally related to attitudes, they do not develop to an efficient degree without attention. In fact, the quality and breadth of communication depend in a large measure on the skills developed by each member. In the beginning very few members have the requisite skills for effective functioning. One has only to observe an inexperienced group to be convinced of the lack of quality in the use of needed skills to maximize the meaningfulness of interaction. Many group members lack such skills as listening, group observation, clarifying, linking, comprehension, analysis, synthesis, interpretation and evaluation.

Some of these skills are much more difficult to develop adequately than others. Some make it necessary for the person exercising the skill to be able to reach objective conclusions. Those who feel threatened find this difficult to do without the distortion of ideas expressed in the group.

Such skills as synthesis, evaluation and interpretation present great difficulty when one is trying to be objective. Also, some skills require concentrated attention over a period of time and the careful mental organization of ideas. The skills of linking, synthesis and summarization present this challenge.

GROUP OBSERVATION[3]

In the beginning members observe and talk to one person. Only gradually do they become accustomed to talking to the whole group. At first their attention is given to hearing the ideas. Members often report difficulty in "keeping up" with the conversation. Later they become able to observe nonverbal behavior, prominent body movements, and finally facial expressions. As they gain this facility they begin to relate words and expressions in order better to understand what the words mean to the speaker. They become aware that members may express an idea or give information which is false to the others, but which represents the truth to the member expressing it. This ability to observe members in relation to their contributions increases greatly the understanding of one another. Eye contact is a useful development toward this understanding.

It is generally accepted that sitting in a circle facilitates better observation and communication. If a member has to lean forward or look around someone to see, he is unlikely to make the effort.

Since much of our understanding and the growth of cohesiveness is dependent upon the improvement of observation, it should not be left to chance. Members can discuss the need for observation and the ways in which it can be improved.

CLARIFICATION

Skill in listening is a prerequisite for useful clarification. Clarification requires intelligent effort. The basic meaning which the member hopes to convey is difficult to grasp among his incompletely formed ideas; it is necessary, however, if clarity and understanding are to prevail. Clarification makes possible a creative searching and the expression of meanings.

In a small group which is discussing relationships with parents, Bill, a high school student, is describing his father:

Bill: My dad is great in anything that has to do with outdoor work. We have a good time cutting the grass, trimming the hedge, painting the garage. But when I tell him that I haven't time for all of this, that I have to use it on getting grades, he is obviously dissatisfied and sometimes lets me know it.

Leader: It is hard for your dad to see that you can't give more time to working outdoors with him.

John: My dad is just the same in an opposite way.

Leader: You mean he has the same attitude but it is about something different.

John: That's it. He considers studying and making good grades just about all I should do and is unhappy when I mention doing something outside.

When the leader clarifies, he encourages the members to express their emerging ideas in the formative stage. They become interested in the way he helps them to improve their understanding and capabilities through discussion.

The discussion moves ahead as the members improve in recognizing what needs clarification and in becoming increasingly able to say briefly what another has attempted to express. The sense of purpose and direction which follows leads to more ideas and clearer concepts.

REFLECTION

Reflection is expressing the meaning of an idea. It is from the meaning of ideas that insights develop. The more accurate the reflection of the meaning, the more self-understanding the member can be expected to attain. Through reflection the understanding of members and leader is enlarged. This results in an increased breadth and depth of relatedness.

However, to capture the meaning and to do so within the framework of the speaker's ideas is a difficult task requiring concentration and practice. When someone says, "I don't understand you," it should not be inferred that the idea that you stated is beyond his grasp. It could be that he senses a depth of meaning in what you say to which he finds it difficult to respond. The deeper meaning which was intended eludes him or he was speaking lightly and his idea was taken seriously.

In a small group discussion about going to a concert, one teenager concludes, "I don't think I want to go, but I guess I might as well. What else is there to do?" One leader might respond, "You feel it is better to go than to do nothing." Another might respond, "You feel dissatisfied that there is nothing more interesting to do." Still another might say, "You see it as a way of keeping from being bored." That leaders respond so differently may be a surprise, but they vary in their ability to understand. Each can only reflect the meaning the idea has for him. Leaders who seldom think deeply about situations and problems are unlikely to catch meaning in depth which is often disguised or only suggested.

The member whose meaning has been sensitively and accurately reflected by another has an encouraging sense of being understood. He feels more that he is a part of the group and accepted as a member in his own right. The way is prepared for his further participation in self-understanding and understanding of others.

Members find this skill difficult to develop, because it requires putting oneself fully at the service of the task. It is born of the commitment to aid another to gain understanding and direction.

INTERPRETATION

It is difficult to distinguish between reflection and interpretation, and in some instances the wall of separation is very thin. One useful guideline is the following: A reflection remains within the meaning of the member's response; an interpretation goes beyond it, presenting ideas which are not included in what the member says.

There is wide variance in the use of interpretation. Leaders differ in their use of interpretation because they differ in their beliefs about the capabilities of members. For some leaders, the act of interpretation is also an important means of satisfying their own ego needs. As a result they differ in their theoretical assumptions regarding the usefulness of interpretations.

The leader who believes that in a climate of genuine acceptance the member is capable of examining himself in depth and will do so, considers an interpretation unnecessary and possibly detrimental. On the other hand, the leader who perceives the members to be largely incapable of examining their experiences may consider interpretation to be a necessary and important responsibility.

One point of difference which affects leaders' practices focuses on the meaning of acceptance. Leaders agree on the significance of acceptance, but they disagree on its meaning. Those who use interpretation consider acceptance within a framework of normal expectancy. It is a broad but conditional acceptance having limits which are marked off by what is acceptable to the particular leader. These use interpretation as a means of involving the member and helping him to gain insight.

Others, especially group-centered leaders, believe in unconditional acceptance and view interpretation as a contradiction to their basic belief and detrimental in its effects.

The risks of those who use interpretations are several. The members may perceive interpretations as an indication of lack of acceptance. Members often react defensively or even with hostility to the attempts to interpret their thoughts, motives or intentions. This can take place regardless of the accuracy of the interpretation. Another risk is that any interpretation may have the effect of conveying an evaluation or a disbelief in the validity of what is said, or an intention to influence another's thoughts or behavior. Research has shown that interpretations are followed by "abandonment of self-exploration" and by "resistance" more frequently than could be expected by chance.

The risk that group-centered leaders run in not using interpretation is the possibility that introspection on the part of the members may not occur frequently or at a level deep enough to induce attitudinal changes.

Recently leaders have made use of interpretation in very different ways. One of these is the leader's explanation and interpretation of his own experiencing. In so doing it is quite possible that the leader may introduce for the members' consideration an attitude, a belief, a behavior, or some information which causes them to examine themselves from a different perspective. Some leaders consider this method useful in stimulating introspection. It may influence some members to respond verbally by describing their attitudes and feelings to other members of the group. It also focuses attention on the acceptability and safety of this kind of searching in the group environment.

Another variation is a member's decision to explain and interpret to the group his present and/or past behavior, beliefs and goals. When the decision to do so is freely the member's, it proves helpful both to the member and to the whole group. If he can be truthful and also feel safe in doing so it appears to help the member to make his own self-directed change, since it publicly commits him to change. This change is more likely to be made and to endure if the member explains and communicates his new attitudes and intentions to those who were most influenced by what he did.

THE "LINKING" FUNCTION[4]

In the discussion of a topic the comments of members may be related to the topic, but their internal relatedness may not be clear. There are at least two reasons for this: (1) the meaning of each comment may be clear but its relatedness to another may be obscure; (2) the comments may be involved, lengthy, and unclear although their relatedness is more evident. In these situations the thought of each member remains independent or unlinked to the expressed ideas of other members. This causes the group to feel at a standstill, lacking a sense of continuity and direction.

If the comments are clear and not involved, the leader may decide only to indicate their interrelatedness. If they are involved, he searches for the meaning of each comment and how these meanings are related. By penetrating the content to its meaning, the leader can recognize the relationship of each new comment to the previous one. He is then able to indicate the ongoing meaning running throughout the separate comments and to convey this to the group. The discussion then becomes clear and each succeeding comment bears a useful relationship to what has gone before. The following excerpt from a meeting of a church board concerned with the finances of the church may help to illustrate the function of linking ideas:

John: I know we don't want to force people to give, but I don't see this talk about trust. I think I could trust you to give your share without solicitation, but that's as far as it goes.

Jean: It's hard for me, too. I think trust is something that you develop when you are a child. If you miss it then, it is more difficult to develop later.

Mary: I am worried about this whole idea. I think I am a trusting person but I was in a church once where they didn't canvass one year and they didn't raise the needed money.

Bob: I think we say something about ourselves and our belief in people when we insist on a canvass, but I find it hard to trust people to give.

Leader: We have some questions about this idea of trusting members to give. We feel perhaps that we should trust but we are not so sure that we can.

Jean: You have to trust people or you and they never grow.

Bill: There is always the first time. I feel that we trust each other now much more than we did a few weeks ago.

Betty: Maybe that's what is holding us up in trying to decide. We are not taking the risk of letting others know what we think.

John: But what's the point in all this? Why not canvass? We know we'll get the money that way.

Harold: I would like to know how the others feel. If we could trust one another to say what we are really thinking we could reach a more satisfactory decision.

Leader: Are we saying that to trust is a risk but a necessary one if we are to understand one another and reach a good decision?

The leader has tried to link and focus the thinking of the group on two occasions. In the first case his response was chiefly a feedback of what the members had said. It served the purpose of helping the group to decide the direction the discussion should take.

In the second instance the leader searched out the thread of meaning basic to the various comments and responded in a manner that placed the central idea before the group. If the leader can do this well, the members have a sense that they are understood, a certainty concerning what they have said, and a realization of progress.

SUMMARIZATION[5]

To summarize well is very difficult. Yet a good summary is a unique and important function in helping the group to recognize the basic ideas they have discussed. Also it provides the members with a sense of direction and aids them in planning next steps. When continuity is important to the purposes of the group, a summary proves invaluable.

A summary may take several forms. An orderly presentation of the key ideas which have been discussed is useful and necessary in educational groups. In a counseling group, a summary which presents the various approaches in the consideration of problems is facilitative. It focuses on possible ways in which each member may try to understand himself and his interpersonal functioning.

A summary may be offered at different times in the group discussion. The leader or member summarizes when he considers it to be helpful to the group. This may be during the discussion—especially if the group is trying to explore its own interpersonal relationships and progress—and also at the close if the aims of the group are educational.

Part of the difficulty experienced in summarizing is a lack of knowledge of what is involved. Also detrimental may be a practice which is haphazard and unintelligent concerning what is required. An analysis of the process indicates that a summarizer performs three operations; he encodes the information which the members present, he stores it, and later retrieves it for their use.

The most important and difficult is the encoding stage. The leader must be able to hear and organize ideas, many of which may not be in accord with his point of view. He suspends his own evaluative process and listens to hear the import of what each member says. To encode the ideas, he penetrates to the meaning of each item and determines which items can be contained under one basic idea.

In the storing stage, he sets up categories. This requires the recognition of a different subject or of a different focus on the same subject, and a decision on the category and meaning it will convey.

As he clearly differentiates and encodes the items, he stores them under their descriptions and proceeds to concentrate on current inputs.

For the purpose of retrieval, he reviews the encoded information in each category as the opportunity presents itself. This helps him to retrieve it in the order and in the form in which he stored it.

CONCLUSIONS

The members and the leader should engage in recognizing, analyzing, and improving present skills and in increasing the range of skills each is able to use. Attention should be given to the development of insight with reference to those skills which are appropriate at various times in the group's progress.

Due recognition should be given to the fact that the quality of the interaction in a group is largely dependent on the skills developed by the leader and members. Such skills can be developed only by continuous and intelligent practice.

5 *THE LEADER*

Qualities of the Leader

The qualities which a leader should possess remain undecided. However, there is agreement that his leadership is a composite result of what he is and what he does. What he is has been obscured by the emphasis authorities place on the skills of leadership. His beliefs, goals, and the meanings by which he lives receive little, if any consideration.

There is not a common denominator for use as a starting point for the examination of leadership qualities. Each author describes the qualities of the leader from his individual perspective. The result in each case is a perception of the leader as viewed through the tenets of the particular discipline in which the author is versed. In many instances this approach tends to set the leader apart from the group and to describe him in terms of only the behavioral sciences.

Teaching, counseling, management, business, medicine and law have their individual conceptions of the qualities which a leader should possess and each differs from the others in some important respects. Differences exist even within a single discipline. Gibb[1] characterizes the qualities of a leader who believes in "defensive" management as different from those of a leader who believes in "participative" management. The qualities of the defensive leader are characterized as "high fear and low trust." Whereas the participative leaders are characterized as persons of "low fear and high trust." Equally different are the qualities of the T-group and group-centered leaders in group counseling.

NEW DIRECTIONS

The qualities of the leader took a new direction with the concept of distributive leadership. Before the advent of democratic leadership the qualities of the leader were assumed to be distinct from those of the members, but the leader of a democratic or group-centered group is viewed as possessing some of the qualities that the members possess, and the members are known to possess some of the same qualities as those possessed by the leader.

Similarities are most obvious in the area of skill-functioning and least obvious in the areas of quality and depth of perception. Both leader and members communicate through such skills as listening, clarification and reflection. Most leaders communicate through these skills more expertly and easily than most members.

The leader's training, experience and heightened sense of responsibility account for the difference in large part. He feels a dedication to assisting each member of the group and a sense of responsibility to each and to the group as a whole. This same attitude of caring and responsibility for the development of the members induces the leader to increase his powers of concentration. His responsibilities demand that he be able to relate and that he formulate the diverse ideas of the members into some pattern and direction. He must also be able to sense to some degree the psychological meaning of each member's response.

It may be that the intangible qualities of the leader influence his leadership more than his skills and his ability to concentrate. These intangible elements are of two kinds: those which have to do with his general patterns of perception and sensitivity and those which are directly related to his understandings of the meaning of life itself.

The perception of the leader is patterned directly by the manner in which he satisfies his ego needs. A leader may satisfy his ego needs through personal achievement and through the honor and status which result. Such a leader is perceptive of the progress of the group toward a goal which he considers desirable. On the other hand, a leader may satisfy his ego needs through the improvement of each member's personality development. Such a leader is perceptive of the nuances of "becoming" expressed in the member's behavior. Each leader emphasizes the method of ego-fulfillment which gives him more satisfaction. Needless to say, the two kinds of leaders will be quite different in their attitudes and methods.

SENSITIVITY

The sensitivity of the leader bears a direct relationship to the kind and depth of his perception. It is further dependent upon his willingness to risk becoming involved in another person's way of looking at life. Sensitivity at its best is the setting aside of one's own preferences and predilections and willingly and unreservedly assimilating another's viewpoints and ideas regarding the important matters that concern him. At its worst sensitivity is learning about a person in order to manipulate him or his environment.

Sensitivity that helps another is best attained by the leader who has security and a personal center. The degree to which the leader is able to understand another is directly related to his self-knowledge and acceptance of himself in all his aspects.

Leaders' attitudes toward members are a function of the character of their sensitivity. Some leaders have both empathy and consideration for members. Ross and Hendry[2] consider these to be among the most significant qualities which the leader may possess. Leaders who are sensitive to the members' values, goals and feelings are able to perceive life from the viewpoint of the members.

The possibility of doing this is enhanced to the degree that the leader is more interested in understanding the member than in changing him. Understanding for the purpose of changing the member in the direction preferred by the leader should be questioned. Such understanding is unlikely to help the member to understand himself and to reset his own goals. Such a relationship may cause him to feel threatened and less able to examine and express his concerns.

CONSIDERATION

The quality of consideration may take several forms. Some leaders are proud of their "consideration" for members (children, students, employees) when they do things for them because the members are "too young," "too inexperienced," or "too busy." They may even consider it their duty to make decisions for a member rather than let him suffer from what the leader likes to think are less adequate alternatives.

Consideration which makes a constructive difference has its roots in understanding and caring. Consideration which results in questionable outcomes is born not of sensitivity, understanding and caring but of the leader's great desire for satisfying his ego needs even at the risk of manipulation.

The character and quality of the leader's perception are basic to his degree of sensitivity as expressed in his empathy and consideration. The quality of the leader's perceptions varies in relation to the degree of his open-mindedness. The open-minded leader is more secure and less threatened. He has little need to narrow and distort his perceptions, is more aware of his reaction to stimuli and is generally able to use more of his psychic energy in self-understanding and in understanding others in the group.

INTANGIBLES

The foregoing description of the qualities of the leader omits the influence of his beliefs, goals and meanings of life. To this extent it is partial and leaves unexamined the essence of his leadership. Let us now turn to these neglected but very significant intangibles.

There are many such intangibles. Only a few will be mentioned and briefly commented upon, but it is hoped they will aid the reader to encompass the various dimensional possibilities of leaders.

One intangible is imagination. The leader relies on it in the examination of his past leadership and in his plans for improvement. Leaders vary in their use of imagination. Some leaders use it to focus on procedures which have been accepted and tried. This use of imagination, which is decidedly limited in its helpfulness to the leader, Jung[3] has called "reproductive." Other leaders use imagination not only in examining the past but in looking at the future. The focus is on a creative expectancy, which permits symbolic meaning. To use imagination in such a purposeful or productive manner is a challenging and threatening endeavor. The leader should recognize that the quality of his work bears a direct relation to the ways in which he uses his imagination for understanding and planning.

Another intangible is the nature of the leader's thinking concerning his leadership. Is his thinking open-ended? Does he entertain and cultivate symbolic thought which is concerned with what is beyond human comprehension or does he think in terms only of the practical, the expedient, the useful? Is he interested only or chiefly in process meanings? If so, group process and his own effort are comprehended by the use of signs only. He finds little need for symbolic thought. To the degree that this is so, an important quality is missing in his leadership. The group experience is adversely affected, because the conditions upon which a high quality of interpersonal relationship and productivity depend (trust, freedom, and responsibility) are symbols. What takes place in the group is limited when members are reduced to signs for communication. Such a leader would consider it wishful daydreaming and impractical to think in terms of what could be possible. He has no place for the acceptance of ambiguity and uncertainty.

A further important intangible is the leader's approach in meeting the exigencies of life. How does he reach decisions personally and in his leadership? How he proceeds is a product of the potentialities which he has developed. Some leaders solve problems and accept the outcomes by asking chiefly the questions of possibility, utility and expediency. These take a pragmatic approach to life.

Some leaders ask these but also other questions, such as: "Is the decision I am about to make helpful to the persons for whom I have responsibility? Is it just? Is it in accord with my beliefs and values?"

All leaders have some characteristics of each classification, but they tend to reach conclusions in terms of one process more than the other. It is very possible that leaders with the same qualifications and experience and using the same general method would intiate and develop widely different value attitudes in their groups. The depth and quality of the group experience would differ in relation to the leader's use of his depth potential in reaching decisions.

. . . AND COURAGE

The leader who develops his potential is one who meets the challenge of each new opportunity with courage. The reference to courage here is not the courage to meet external threats but an inward quality, a way of relating to oneself and one's possibilities. Kurt Goldstein views it as an affirmative answer to the shocks of existence, which must be borne to actualize one's own nature.

True courage helps the leader to mature. If he acts courageously only because it is the expected thing to do, or if he does so under the dominance of authority figures, he does not develop inner courage. In other words, true courage is one of the functions of a strong personal center. A leader who possesses it trusts his insights. He is also able to examine critically his performance as a leader and his beliefs and values regarding life's meaning. He rededicates himself to new insights which evolve as the result of his evaluations.

Paul Tillich[4] describes true courage as the "courage to be." Such a leader recognizes, accepts, develops and believes in his own potentialities. Many leaders approach this but remain only with the "courage to be as a part." This courage frequently succumbs to the vicissitudes of life such as tragedy, a destructive fate, a breakdown of convictions, guilt and momentary despair. The leader with true courage feels neither destroyed nor condemned by these. He makes experiments in accordance with his best judgment. He expects and accepts risks and failures, and even some catastrophes. Leaders who are most useful are able to take such anxieties into themselves and transcend them to achieve greater understanding and sensitivity.

How the Leader Functions

The leader hopes to improve the quality of interpersonal behavior. He views himself as a facilitator of behavioral change. The methods he uses to induce change are a function of his beliefs regarding how change takes place. Democratic and group-centered leaders function from within the group as special members. In T groups, sensitivity groups and encounter groups, the leader functions from outside the group; he is not perceived as a group member.

IN AN INTERDEPENDENT RELATIONSHIP

The leader is in an interdependent relationship. He cannot be fully understood apart from the group and both are affected by the interaction.The members expect him to improve the social milieu and widen the field of participation. They respect his leadership to the extent that it satisfies sufficiently their self-perceived needs.

These needs vary greatly with groups. If the majority of the members in a group desire structure, precision and preplanning, they will be relatively more satisfied and secure if the leader plans and explains. If, on the other hand, the majority of the members are open to experience, able to accept and appreciate the challenge of the new, and will tolerate ambiguity with little difficulty, they will support a leader who engages with them in this kind of experience.

IMPORTANT DECISIONS

The leader makes important and sometimes difficult decisions both when the group sessions commence and during their progress. One of these decisions is concerned with the kind and quantity of structure. The leader makes this decision within the context of his special method of working with groups and his judgment concerning the reaction of the members who comprise the group. A T-group leader and a group-centered leader will probably make different decisions.

A second decision focuses on the problem of who will be accepted in the group. Will it be a homogeneous group concerned with some common problems or a heterogeneous group with a random sample of concerns? If his decision is in favor of a heterogeneous group, what criteria will be used in setting up the group? Will the group be heterogeneous on the basis of age, interests or attitudes? If homogeneous, what method will be used in the acceptance of enrollees to ensure the degree of homogeneity desired?

A third decision revolves around the problem of commitment. In order to attain the greatest degree of usefulness, members need to attend the group sessions regularly. Many leaders require a commitment to do so from each member as a condition for enrollment. Other leaders ask for a commitment but only after the member has attended one, two or three sessions.

A fourth decision closely related to the third is the number of meetings. Groups meet for varying periods of times. Some groups, known as marathon groups, meet continuously for fifteen hours, twenty-four hours or a weekend, with time out for rest and food. Something can be accomplished in groups meeting once or twice a week, from one to two and a half hours, for six weeks. However, most leaders think of a minimum of ten meetings totaling at least twenty-five hours. When groups can meet for longer times, it is reasonable to expect that more will be gained from the experience.

A fifth decision concerns the nature of the groups. Will the leader conduct an educational group or a counseling group? This is a crucial decision and most leaders do not try to decide this independently. Instead they clarify all expectations with the members. It is extremely unfortunate when the members expect an educational experience and the leader tries to involve them in therapy instead.

Some leaders—especially those who are group-centered—consider it important and useful to explain to the members their ideas regarding how people change and how these ideas are applied in the process in which they will be involved. The leader helps them to understand what to expect from him and what he expects from them. If this varies too much from a member's expectation, the leader should make it possible for that person to leave the group without embarrassment.

Other decisions which the leader makes concern the size of the group, the place of meeting, the length of each meeting, the feasibility of subgroups, and methods of evaluation.

ORGANIZATION

An important function of the leader is to organize the group. Depending on the situation, the leader may interview each member previous to the commencement of the group sessions. Interviews are valuable if the leader wants to select personally the kinds of persons to be in the group. He might, for instance, believe that he needs verbal, nonverbal, idea-oriented, and feeling-oriented persons in order to create the balance that will best serve the purposes of all.

Some leaders believe that a group composed of members who differ from one another in some degree with regard to their values and attitudes has greater possibilities for growth than a homogeneous group. Such leaders may use some kind of opinionnaire in order to form groups or subgroups whose members are interesting to one another. This author has found opinionnaires valuable.

Members find it easier to begin by relating to a few other members and then gradually increasing the number to whom they relate. A method used by some leaders is to separate the large group into groups of three for a part of each meeting time; then into groups of five, seven, nine, and finally the total group for the full time. Members often prefer to spend part of each meeting in a small group and part in the total group.

Each group needs information to help the members with understanding the process and their own functioning within it. Also they need to consider the application of the process to their interpersonal relationships in the home, among friends, and in church, club and work situations. Some leaders supply the information which they perceive is needed through lectures given apart from the group-process experience. This is the usual method of leaders using the T-group method. Group-centered and democratic-group leaders incorporate discussions of informational content as it is needed. This may be incorporated into the discussion itself or added at its close.

Regardless of his method a leader may encourage and participate in ongoing observations and evaluations of the process. In some groups observations and evaluations are made chiefly by the leader (as in T groups). In other groups observers selected by the group do this, assisted by the leader and members of the group. In group-centered and democratic groups the function of evaluation is more generally distributed among the members and the leader.

PARTICIPATION

Each leader sets the tone of the process in his group. If the leader is permissive and accepting, if he listens carefully to each member, if he observes the members of the group, the members take their cue from him and gradually do likewise.

On the other hand, if he interprets, if he makes suggestions, if he accepts only within limits, if he presses members to participate in certain ways, the members in this situation also take their cue from him and gradually do likewise. The leader is an example to the group. To some degree he illustrates what each of them considers a guide.

Leaders do more than this. They immerse themselves in the interaction among the members. They observe and listen to each member with great concentration. They do so in order better to understand the dynamics of what is taking place, and in order to understand each member as much as possible. This understanding is necessary if the leader is to facilitate the group's progress.

How the leader tries to facilitate the progress of the group varies with his beliefs regarding how this may take place. Progress in group process is indicated by increasing openness and readiness of the members to personalize their comments; to discuss the "here and now" of what is taking place; to entertain creative differences of thought, belief and action among the members; to tolerate the ambiguity which ensues from the limitations to know and be known; to accept responsibility for the maintenance and ongoing development of the group; and to share in the responsibility of helping one another to further one's becoming.

Leaders believe that these conditions result from contrasting sets of conditions. Group-centered and democratic leaders believe that these conditions result from a psychological climate which provides the needed safety and acceptance for members to be what they really are. In an environment in which fear and threat are minimal, these leaders expect members gradually to become able to involve themselves and to do so at increasingly deeper levels of their experience. These leaders rely on clarification, reflection and acceptance responses with occasional summarization as deemed necessary.

T-group, sensitivity-group, and basic-encounter-group leaders rely on a very different set of conditions. They do not believe that conditions based on unconditional acceptance will induce members to become sufficiently involved for behavioral change to take place. Therefore they perform in such a way as to increase ambiguity, frustration and anxiety in order to secure the involvement they believe necessary.

Leaders hope that members will reality-test their developing ideas and attitudes. They view the group environment as the ideal place for members to try out their new ways of thinking and acting. By so doing each member gains assurance of his acceptance and improves his self-image. Leaders in congruence with their patterns of functioning support and encourage the members to engage in reality-testing.

In varying degrees leaders assist members to transfer their new attitudes and viewpoints to life outside the group. They encourage members to use their productive imaginations to understand how to relate to others in terms of their new perspectives, attitudes and skills. Members need help in recognizing that the community and communication they have experienced in the group may be very different from that in their social and work relationships. The more the group departs from the usual ways of relating to others, the more difficult it can be for members to use their new self-concepts and feelings profitably in other situations.

Types of Leadership Functioning[5]

Leaders perform differently because they believe in different methods and have varying needs for ego satisfaction.[6] The latter in part explains why two authoritarian leaders may perform somewhat differently and with dissimilar results. Since the characteristics and behavior of leaders differ widely, the types of leadership[7] will be clarified and described below.

It is hoped that the brief descriptions of each type of leadership will help to emphasize the important differences in their functioning.

AUTHORITARIAN

The authoritarian leader plans, informs and directs. He decides the goals to be achieved or accepts those which are given him. He tries to motivate the group to accept them and to use his suggestions, requests or demands.

He centers control in himself through various forms of evaluation and the use of reward, praise or fear of punishment. He assumes that his decisions are superior to those of the group and perceives his function as one of directing the members toward the fixed goals. He uses his authority to secure compliance to his wishes and expects a high degree of conformity. His decisions are based on his assumption that the group is inexperienced, untrained or uninformed about the matter under consideration.

Those authorities who accept this point of view commend leaders who are forceful, energetic, capable planners, efficient organizers, and successful in getting group members to perform. A good leader influences members to vote for him, work for him, and give him token respect.

Although some members welcome the security this structure establishes, there are certain problems. Some apparently recognize that they are sacrificing their right to share in the making of decisions. Such persons may sabotage the plans, suggestions or requirements demanded and become very restrictive in their responses. Others react by passivity, conformity, withdrawal or "apple polishing." Hostility, directed toward the leader or other members, occurs frequently. This may produce counterhostility, cliques or various kinds of subgroups which may undermine the leader's authority.

If the authoritarian leader is successful he may at least provide for a number of the members: (1) a feeling of identification with a significant person, (2) a sense of security (pseudo perhaps), and (3) a sense of achievement.

DEMOCRATIC

The democratic leader engages in cooperative planning and functioning. He involves himself in this in accordance with the freedom in the situation, or the "unfixed ends," his own security and experience and that of the group.

He helps members to clarify their interests and goals and to select a problem of mutual concern. He further helps them to focus their highest quality of thinking on the situation. Through their experience they produce a result which may be concrete or ideational in form.

The democratic leader carefully develops and respects the evaluative abilities of the group members. The controls and direction are developed cooperatively. He aids the members in the visualization of alternatives and the projection of themselves into the ensuing situations, the result of which is the choice of an alternative. In relation to their particular training and experience he assumes that the members of the group are as capable as he is in making decisions.

He uses his status for the improvement of the quality of thinking and behavior. He accomplishes this through listening, questioning, reacting, and, when necessary, by reflection, clarification and synthesis. In this manner he helps the members to focus their thinking on the situation. He assumes that free, thoughtful reflection and interaction among the members will produce better decisions.

Persons who accept this point of view consider good leaders to be those who facilitate an environment conducive to freedom of expression, who respect the personality of each individual and understand the meaning of his verbal expression, and who act as a resource person and aid in the development of each group member.

The democratic leader may experience certain difficulties in: (1) permitting the members the right to evaluate; (2) recognizing situations with "unfixed ends" and using them for growth purposes; (3) appraising judiciously the ability and readiness of the members for democratic planning; (4) developing situational thinking as a prerequisite to cooperative planning; (5) assisting members to modify their stereotypic concept of the leader's role; (6) encouraging member interaction, which is essential to cooperative planning.

His reasonable success in the accomplishment of these could be expected to have the following results in the group: (1) greater ability to cooperate; (2) a higher quality of thinking; (3) more self-reliance, responsibility and control in carrying out decisions; and (4) more understanding of self, of others, and of the democratic process.

GROUP-CENTERED

The primary emphases of this leader are: (1) the release of each member's potential capacities; and (2) the development of independence and self-responsibility within each member. The group-centered leader's functioning stems from his belief in self-theory. Two tenets of this theory are the following: (1) a "climate" of unconditional acceptance is most conducive to behavioral change; and (2) a person genuinely changes when he is free not to change. The leader therefore perceives his function to be that of helping the group to work out its own functioning and by so doing to become more responsible.

He encourages the following conditions: (1) a nonthreatening, accepting psychological climate; (2) the absence of barriers within and among all members of the group; and (3) an increasing opportunity for participation.

He is warm and empathic, and he listens to each member to understand the meaning of that person's contribution. He does not evaluate comments; he accepts, clarifies, synthesizes, reflects and summarizes. He encourages permissiveness within the limits of the situation.

He meets with certain problems in the initiation and furtherance of this kind of leadership: (1) Some progress has to be made before he loses the stereotypic leader role and is accepted as a member of the group. Then, in the manner of any other member, his ideas or plans will be evaluated, accepted or rejected. (2) He may be unable to assess accurately and wisely the members' characteristics in preparing the group for their new experience. (3) A proportion of the group membership may be unable to accept the leader on an equal, nonauthoritative basis. (4) Increasing member participation develops only through the accepting climate; it cannot be forced or verbally encouraged.

To the degree that the undertaking is successful, the following outcomes can be expected: (1) members accept responsibility for evaluation; (2) members develop skills in group functioning; (3) members feel that they are accepted and understood; (4) members change from ego-centered to group-centered thinking and participation; (5) spontaneous expressions and reality-testing increase; and (6) dependence on the leader decreases and a responsibility toward one another and for the welfare of the group increases.

T GROUP [8]

The trainer of the T group plans for the total involvement of the members through a discussion of what is currently taking place in the attitudes and feelings of the group members. In doing so he uses ambiguity and frustration as a means of increasing and heightening involvement. He intervenes in the discussion, using suggestions, questions, advice, interpretation and information-giving to direct the group in accordance with his preplanned goals.

The trainer is confronted by certain questions as he initiates and carries out his leadership role: (1) How much ambiguity and frustration are useful as a means of increasing involvement? At what point do they become so disruptive that their usefulness is questionable? (2) To what degree is the lecture helpful as a means of supplying cognitive input? Does its use increase intellectualization more than is desirable? (3) How much emphasis should be placed on the "here and now" in relation to the "there and then" thinking of the group? (4) Should the trainer remain outside the group, become a member of the group, or be a member only during certain phases of the group experience?

To the degree that the trainer is successful, he can expect the following: (1) a reduction in the defenses of the members; (2) an increase in the ability of the members to perceive and learn from the consequences of their actions; (3) an increased understanding of group functioning; (4) an acceptance of responsibility for the reduction of barriers to communication within themselves; and (5) an ability not only to give help but also to receive it from others.

SUMMARY

Each method of leadership is based on different assumptions, procedures and outcomes. Some members benefit most from one kind of group, other members from a different kind of group. The leader alone does not develop a useful group; it requires the cooperative effort of both leader and members. The chief differences can be placed under three headings: the locus of the problem, the locus of procedure and the locus of evaluation.

In authoritarian leadership the locus of the problem and the locus of evaluation are within the leader. In democratic leadership the problem is selected cooperatively and evaluation is made by the members assisted by the leader. In group-centered leadership both the selection of the problem and the evaluation are centered in the members. In T-group leadership the locus of the problem is within the leader with some lessening as the group gains experience.

When a group has an authoritarian leader interaction is two-way. He initiates and continues the discussion. Questions are answered by him, and ideas are presented directly to him. In a democratic group there is a cooperative relationship and a respect for one another's ideas. There is a three-way interaction from leader to members, from members to leader, and from one member to another. In the group-centered group the procedure is initiated and continued by the members. Leader and members accept one another regardless of one another's contribution or lack of it. This acceptance is emphasized by the leader who does not give advice, interpret, or make suggestions. In the T group the trainer questions, encourages and directly or indirectly evaluates. The trainer maintains the direction of the process; two-way interaction is the norm.

Leaders' Problems Today

CHALLENGE OF THE NEW

The advent of different approaches in group process emphasizes the ever-present need for leader self-examination. It is necessary not only that the leader understand the foundational principles of each method but also that he understand himself in relation to them.

He also needs to be aware of the changing perceptions of group members. The impingement of emerging societal mores decreases the sense of stability and security in the areas of ideas, values and behavior. Ideological conflicts, distant and near at hand, influence interpersonal relationships in subtle and disturbing ways.

On the other hand, new viewpoints and different questions increase tremendously the possibilities of discovering things old and new through open, candid interaction in small groups. The success of such experience depends to a large degree on the leader's willingness and readiness to relate to the members. Members are asking new questions in a sincere endeavor to discover meaning as well as symbols through which to give expression to the experience.[9]

It is therefore important that the leader confront the problems of leadership today. These problems may be examined from the perspectives of his source of ego satisfaction, motivation and congruence.

EGO SATISFACTION

He could begin with the question: "What is the source of my ego satisfaction in my work with groups?" He may find that his chief satisfaction springs from offering useful suggestions and upon occasion giving advice, making logical analyses, providing excellent summaries, and involving the members through the use of some technique. If these are his sources of satisfaction, then what method of group process would he enjoy the most, and in which would he provide the most useful leadership? Such a leader should seriously question group-centered leadership as his choice unless he is willing to change genuinely.

On the other hand, the leader may discover that to analyze, question, suggest, encourage, reinforce and evaluate are distasteful to him and that he is uneasy when he does these things. This type of leader senses a great delight when a member becomes less defensive, more verbal, gains new insight, or apparently becomes more relaxed in the group. Such a leader receives ego satisfactions from the change which the member makes rather than from the demonstration of his own capability as a leader. This leader should seriously consider a choice of the T group, basic encounter group, or some other similarly based theoretical method unless he is willing to change.

Of course, the derivation of the ego satisfactions of leaders cannot be validly separated into such convenient categories. Generally it is a matter of degree, but the leader interested in knowing can discern whether his satisfactions are based chiefly on what happens to him or on what happens to the members.

PROBLEM OF MOTIVATION

A second kind of introspection the leader makes is concerned with member motivation. He examines his practices to determine whether he relies upon extrinsic or intrinsic motivation. He tries to discern to what degree he uses reinforcement, advice, suggestions, analysis, interpretation, mild persuasion or reward to induce members to perform as he perceives they should. If occasionally he relies upon intrinsic motivation, what difficulty does he experience and what degree of doubt does he feel? Does he rely upon intrinsic motivation consistently or only occasionally when the hoped-for outcomes are not crucial?

Such examination will help the leader to recognize his convictions regarding what induces behavioral change. It will help him to understand his own behavior and that of the members.

If he believes that change in behavior results from influences upon the members such as rewards, reinforcement, suggestion or persuasion, he should perform in this way. He should become knowledgeable and skilled in the methods of the authoritarian group, T group or basic encounter group.

However, if he believes change in behavior originates within the member, the leader should do what he can to create a climate of unconditional acceptance. He should become knowledgeable and skilled in the method of the group-centered group.

PROBLEM OF CONGRUENCE

The leader is congruent when he knows his convictions regarding behavioral change and acts in accordance with them. Congruence is not gained by an intellectual exercise alone; it is a total intentionality. The leader desires to be congruent but may find this difficult.

He frequently falls short of attaining it in one or more of the following ways. He may engage in "party-line" thinking; that is, he compartmentalizes. In this manner he limits conscious communication among incongruent, theoretical ideas. On the other hand, he may maintain communication but in doing so ignore or distort certain aspects of one theory which irreconcilably challenge aspects of another. This kind of difficulty becomes apparent in the widely used word *permissiveness.* Group leaders of several orientations claim to be encouraging permissiveness; however, in practice the meanings of the word vary so widely that they differ not only in degree but also in kind.

The fact that some methods of group process do not have a unified theoretical base presents a dilemma. For example, Rogers describes the basic encounter group as based on Lewinian, psychoanalytical and other theories. Since these present in part diverse positions regarding behavioral change, the leader is in difficulty regarding which position to embrace.

Such multi-theory groups present another problem in congruence. Can the leader accept contrasting and contradictory points of view? If he accepts the theory that genuine change takes place when the individual is free to do otherwise, can he also accept a contradictory theory that genuine change takes place through reinforcement?

Recognizing that individuals differ widely in the conditions which initiate, increase and deepen their involvement, can the leader subscribe to only one method? Should and does he avoid this issue by assuming that if a particular method works, it is good and further examination of it is unnecessary? If so, can he justify such a completely pragmatic approach?

Some group leaders are incongruent in a different sense. If they do not know what they believe, they may be incongruent in their performance in the group. In one situation, they may be analytical, interpretative and accepting in a very limited sense, but at another time they may reflect, clarify and accept unconditionally. They are inconsistent because they have no standards by which to appraise their behavior. This inconsistency deters the members in understanding the leader. They may finally conclude that the leader is basically congruent in satisfying the same psychological needs each time but that he does so in different ways. If members question the leader, he may be at a disadvantage for he has no satisfactory basis by which to explain his action.

The leader who remains incongruent in his theoretical beliefs decreases the possibility of genuineness in his relationships with the group members. To be genuine he needs to know what he believes and to be willing to express his beliefs when doing so would be useful to the group. If he does not recognize the incongruence of the theories on which his action is based, he is unlikely to recognize the problems of the members.

The wise leader will integrate his thinking and action. He will keep them related and he will not adopt a method only because he finds it satisfactory. He will carefully analyze his process and determine to the degree possible the theory or theories on which it is based. He must also determine whether or not his intellectual conclusions are congruent with what he believes about human nature and how change takes place.

Not only should he clarify the nature of the theory which he accepts, but he also needs to examine the degree to which his method exemplifies the theory. If he finds that his method is not in accordance with the basic tenets of the theory he accepts, he should re-examine both in order to attain congruence between his beliefs and his action.

Some leaders try to find firm ground by maintaining an eclectic position in which they assert belief in all theories and use the method of any theory which suits the occasion. But since the theories on which they base their various methods are not supplementary and are frequently at odds with one another, they face a dilemma. Such leaders often arrive at a working semblance of unity by modifying the meaning of the various theoretical positions. In so doing the meanings are made to conform to their predetermined position, which is usually authoritarian in some form and to varying degrees.

Although leaders experience problems in using the right skills at the proper times, their chief problems are existential. The leader finds himself asking, "Who am I?" and "Who are the members?" He is thus engaged in the ongoing discovery of his self-identity and in trying to understand the "being" of the members. "What do I believe?" and "What am I doing?" are the questions at the center of his becoming, both as a person and as a leader.

6 *THE GROUP MEMBER*

What Each Member Contributes[1]

The leader alone cannot change a collection of individuals into a group.[2] He may be interested and he may have the ability to understand the group process but he needs the help of the members. Unless he has their help the favorable atmosphere he initiates will degenerate into the competitive levels often found in a classroom. Members need to be interested and willing to learn how to contribute their part.[3] Group quality emerges from the interaction of members and must be nurtured by everyone.

NECESSARY INSIGHTS

Individuals interested in becoming members of a group should consider the following general basic points.

1. Each member recognizes that the feeling tone or group quality or atmosphere is made by people. It evolves as they relate to one another in working on some area of need which disturbs them.

2. Each member perceives himself as necessary and a referent in the same need situation. Each member transcends his existing point of view by relating it to or modifying it by that of others.

3. He knows that the adequate resolution of a need lies in the interactions of people. He comes to know that the qualitative atmosphere of a group is a product of the psychological interaction of person and person, each of whom is willing and able to change.

4. Each member recognizes that he impedes progress

if he is unwilling to modify his prior perceptions[4] through interaction at any time. He does this, since he structures the whole matter in a fixed direction which tends to prevent the emergence of groupness. Generally the member who denies creative insight in himself is unwilling to admit it or allow it in others.

5. Each member brings to the situation threats from other pseudo-group experiences. He must therefore work to reduce these threats and their influences in himself and others. To the degree that each is able to do so he will become free to modify his perceptions of ideas and things. It will then follow that his new perceptions will have more realistic value to the need.

6. Each member recognizes that high feeling tone is maintained by the sustained effort to manage adequately a common area of disturbance. Sometimes situations outside the group help the group in attaining its goal.

7. Each member gradually recognizes that members with heterogeneous abilities and experiences can contribute more toward emergent group quality than the same number of individuals with relatively homogeneous backgrounds and experiences. The greater the spread of ability and experience in relation to the matter under consideration, the greater the possibility for extending and clarifying perceptions of the parts in relation to a total concern in each member's thinking and feeling. For this to succeed well, each member must be free to release his ideas, meanings and values to the group as he sees them for the interaction of others as they understand them.

MEMBER CONTRIBUTIONS

More specifically, to achieve this group relationship each member studies his behavior and performs certain services. These are described as follows:

1. Each member accepts a common topic, area of disturbance or need on which to work. He does this although it may not be his first or most pressing choice. He assists the group to move along in the formulated direction. His own need, related to this concern formulated by the group, becomes a part of the total experience but not a dominating control. He is ready to learn that his self-discipline in the interest of the larger group quality brings greater benefit to everyone, including himself.

2. He helps the group locate the key emphasis of the discussion and clarifies his own individual need in relation to it. He focuses the major difficulty and works on it until a new direction emerges. He does not permit himself to present unrelated material but holds himself to the points of issue at hand. He is constantly trying to refine his responsibility to the other members of the group, knowing that in the end this will give him the greatest outlet for his own creative energy.

3. He is always willing to revise his thinking in the light of the dynamics of the situation. He does not push toward a previously determined conclusion. Instead he searches for creative insight within the group.

4. He encourages each member to be himself. He accepts the feeling tone of each, the deeper sentiments and the ideas which are an expression of the member's real self. He accepts the sincerity of others although he may not agree with them. His respect for the personhood of each individual helps to create new insights and to enable each self to develop into a constructively contributing member.

5. He concentrates upon the direction the discussion takes. This gives him a sense of how best to contribute. He tries to locate and examine all factors pertinent to each

situation and to learn from experience. This enables him to understand conflict, to assist in the reduction of tensions and to give freedom to everyone for need fulfillment.

6. He tries to prevent or minimize the conditions which might operate against the high level of quality which he and others are striving to reach. The worst condition is that of fear. Members tend to fear those whom they do not understand. These may be people in authority or those with greater ability and more ideas or those with fewer ideas who achieve their ends by subversive means. People fear that their own ideas and meanings will not be accepted by other members. Some may fear change of any sort. Some or all of these fears are present in any group. They are difficult dynamics to change in developing group quality. It requires patient constructive effort by each member, with the help of an understanding, skilled leader to release energy constructively on higher levels.

A high quality of group interaction doesn't just happen. But members working intelligently and responsibly with the help of the leader can gradually bring it about. The members and leader first experience this quality of interrelatedness as a good feeling tone, a happy place to be, a great personal belongingness and status. As the atmosphere of at-homeness increases, the group discusses the basic dynamics and how to apply them in varied life situations.

How Group Members Function

No two members of a group perform in the same way. A member's performance is directly related to the psychological needs he tries to satisfy, his skills in group process and the stage in the development of the group. Each member functions differently as the members progress in becoming a group.

MEMBERS FUNCTION DIFFERENTLY

Each brings to the group his past experiences as well as his expectations in interpersonal relationships. Most members come to the group experience both wanting it and fearing it. For some this natural resistance is soon overcome, but for others it disappears very gradually. There are, of course, both active and passive ways of holding new experiences at bay. The discovery that the usual sources of fear and rivalry are not a part of the group experience helps each member to relax and to begin to drop his defenses.

Some members soon develop interest in the group experience and receive satisfaction from their participation in it. They are generally "other-oriented" in their needs. They move into interpersonal experiences with the expectation that it will have a satisfying outcome. They become interested in others as persons, in understanding them and in helping to make the situation an enjoyable one for all.

GENERAL FUNCTIONS

Various functions of group members have been classified by Benne and Sheats[3] as *group task roles* and *group building and maintenance roles.* Group task roles are related to the task which the group is deciding to undertake or has undertaken. The members facilitate and coordinate group effort in the selection and definition of a common problem and in the solution of that problem. Group building and maintenance roles are oriented toward the functioning of the group as a group. Members are involved in maintaining the group through working, strengthening, regulating and perpetuating the group as a group.

In the beginning of the group experience, members are usually skilled in performing only a few functions, such as asking questions or providing information. Other ways of contributing to the success of the group task are developed through analysis of group performance and intelligent practice. Although any one member may not function in all the roles described below, together most of these ways of contributing will be carried out.

SPECIALIZED FUNCTIONS

One function is that of the *initiator-contributor.* The member may suggest new ways of looking at the matter under discussion or offer a solution to the difficulty or conflict which the group has encountered. Another function is that of the *orienter.* A member may assist the group by indicating that the group has strayed from its original goal or topic. He may also raise questions about the direction the members wish the discussion to take. A third function is that of the *information-giver.* In this case a member offers facts or generalizations, or relates his own experience to the group problem. A fourth function is that of the *elaborator.* He enlarges upon the idea of another member, offers a rationale for opinions or suggestions previously made, or he may describe how an idea or suggestion might work out if adopted by the group. A fifth function is that of the *coordinator.* He shows or clarifies the relationships among various ideas and suggestions and tries to pull them together.

FUNCTIONING OF OTHER-ORIENTED MEMBERS

Other-oriented members, who are not concerned about themselves, assist in building group morale and a sense of belonging. One way in which they do this is in careful listening to another's point of view. A second way is by acceptance of creative differences; that is, the acceptance of ideas and feelings very different from their own. A third way is in helping members to examine their group process and to establish higher levels of aspiration. A fourth way is in helping members toward increasing acceptance of responsibility. This becomes evident in the quality of their interpersonal relationships. Each gradually becomes a person and is accepted on the basis of his personhood rather than for his contribution to the group.

FUNCTIONING OF SELF-ORIENTED MEMBERS

Some members develop interest in others in the group and in the group's activity very slowly and seemingly with great difficulty. They are self-oriented in their needs and much of the time are part of the problem instead of part of the answer in the development of a group.

Each member has a mental picture of a minimum pattern for himself, a sort of personal "height-weight" chart by which he measures himself. If he falls below par in his own estimation, he becomes a problem in the furtherance of group process. He then does what he perceives necessary to improve his self-image. What he does to get "up to par" may not always be acceptable to the group. He may talk too much, or he may not talk at all. He may oppose what someone else suggests just to show himself that he has the strength to oppose the other fellow. The members can help him through their respect for his ideas, even though they may not agree with him. This is not easy for members to do. It requires insight, understanding and self-control, all of which are learned only gradually.

Some members may have strong need to "belong," but are unable to accept the indications of other members that they are wanted. These are so much concerned with their confused feelings that their own thinking never emerges. Only gradually do they come to feel that they are wanted and that they belong. The members—and especially the leader—can try to help each person to feel that he does belong, whether or not his ideas or behavior are similar to those of the group. The leader protects each member's right to be himself, including the right to contribute verbally or not as he desires.

Some members are very uncomfortable in a cooperative situation. It is outside their experience, since cooperative planning discards, to a large extent, this leader-follower concept and implies that all get together on an equal basis. This is difficult for those with strongly self-oriented needs. It asks them to rearrange their mental picture, and this is never easy.

For still others becoming a member takes considerable time and extended experience in a cooperative-planning atmosphere. They may resist strongly being thrown out of role. The person who feels he ought to be boss may try to act as leader or take over the leadership. He may talk too much, act aggressively or be autocratic in his actions and suggestions. The person who feels he ought to be a follower may try to be inconspicuous, refuse to enter into discussion, or claim that group planning is inefficient. In other words, he tries to enact the follower, which is his comfortable role.

Among the best aids in group planning are time and experience. It may help if the "boss" is given some assurance that his ideas are important to the group, and if the "follower" is assured that he is not being presumptuous in expressing an idea.

Each member should try to understand the actions of others by trying to understand the mental pictures of others and thus create a helpful psychological climate. As the members are able increasingly to understand the purpose of group action, how it operates, and how each individual can find his place in it, the group will become more unified.

It should be recognized that the psychological needs of some members arise outside the group in which they find themselves. Some of these needs may be long-standing and the cause of such feeling cannot always be corrected within the group. The group, however, may be of considerable assistance to a member in helping him to understand the sources of his needs, and hence help him in his psychological development. In fact the group must find ways to meet some of the unfulfilled needs of its members.

Some members try to satisfy needs by behaving in certain ways. The leader and members need to recognize these and assist the members as much as possible in developing their sense of belonging and their ability to work cooperatively.

FUNCTIONING OF MEMBERS WITH PROBLEMS

Behavior problems often become apparent early in the life of the group before there is the opportunity to know the member well or understand the basic reasons for their existence. Typical of such behavior patterns are (1) the failure to make any verbal contribution; (2) too much talking; (3) continually wandering from the subject; (4) lagging far behind in learning cooperative techniques; and (5) enjoying conflict for its own sake.

Let us briefly examine each in turn:

1. The silent member may not contribute for various reasons. Perhaps he is afraid to talk before the group. Or maybe he is unable to keep up with the flow of the discussion. It may be that he is not able to formulate his ideas quickly

enough, partly because he has to evaluate their adequacy before he utters them. In former experiences his ideas may have suffered because of the evaluation of other members. Or he may have concluded that he learns more when he just listens and has not yet developed a sense of responsibility to the group.

The method of encouraging interaction in small groups of three or five may be helpful to some of the members with these kinds of difficulties. As members improve in their listening and cease to evaluate, some of them may be encouraged to verbalize. In their self-reports on each session they frequently express difficulty with the pace of the discussion. The leader who reads these anonymous self-reports can bring this to the attention of the members and plans can be made to slow down. As the group climate becomes more accepting most members lessen the degree to which they censure their thoughts before speaking them.

2. The member who talks too much may be only trying to be helpful and not realize that he is monopolizing the time. He may be so uncomfortable by silences in a discussion that he rushes in to fill the gap. Maybe he knows more about the topic and realizes that he does, but does not realize that this is not a license to usurp the rights of others. Or unfortunately he just thinks he knows more than the others—which is another matter. Some people use talk as a defense mechanism to hide their feelings of inadequacy. Some may project their own needs into almost any topic and overdo their enthusiasm with ideas that are not really helpful. A few may need to exert their influence on the group in order to seem important.

It is not easy to help the few who talk too much to improve their usefulness to the group. The leader can be careful to set a good example by careful listening and by making his infrequent contributions concise and relevant. The members can help one another become aware of the importance and necessity of sharing the time in their evaluation sessions either during, or more frequently at the close of, each period. The talkative member might on occasion be listened to attentively by the members for as long as he wishes to talk. This helps the member to feel accepted. Almost without exception this results in the talkative member reducing the length and frequency of his contributions, which as they become less frequent are more likely to become more relevant and useful.

3. The wanderer is the member who seems unable to relate his contribution to the matter under discussion. This behavior may result from several causes. Perhaps the purpose of the discussion is not clear to him. Or perhaps the group shifted to another topic or phase without his recognition of the fact. Maybe he is asked to deal with abstract things when he understands only the more concrete situations. Or the discussion may bore him and he is unwilling to help others who appear to be interested. He may be wandering because he is trying to appear important, to impress the group, rather than to deal with the matter under discussion. In the evaluation members are likely to express disapproval concerning tendencies of others to wander from the subject of discussion. Members are inclined to do something about this kind of deviation.

4. The "slow-to-learn" member may view the use of cooperative techniques as a giving-in to others, as a loss of influence. Or he may fear having to assume some responsibilities if he involves himself completely in cooperative group planning. He may always have been in an environment in which he was told what to do. He may hope to remain secure by conforming to the world which he knows and which is far removed from that of cooperative group process.

He can be expected to change only gradually if the

change is to be genuine. He may be helped by the comments of the group members regarding how the group is trying to operate. He is not put under any pressure to change and he finds that everyone has a place in the process. These conditions may encourage him to be more open and may succeed in interesting him in becoming a true member of the group.

5. There is the member who enjoys conflict for its own sake. Sometimes a member is uneasy unless there is open conflict and disagreement or probing of one another's personal views. Such a member thrives on psychological nudity, especially that of others. Frequently a member who has previously participated in a T group or a basic encounter group feels that nothing worthwhile is taking place without this kind of activity. Such a member is frequently negative and remains apart from any outcome which would require his commitment.

A member may have been conditioned to expect that significant change cannot take place without conflict. Discussion, reasoning, examination of alternatives and compromise are foreign to his experience. He is frequently impulsive, views the world in terms of black and white and also possesses few skills necessary for the examination of contrasting points of view. This is especially true of the culturally deprived of all ages.

He usually has stereotypes of those with dissimilar backgrounds and points of view. This kind of thinking makes his problems of becoming a constructively contributing group member unique.

Such a member is particularly trying to the group. This is so since he continually tests the leader and the other members in an attempt to prove that his stereotypes are correct or to prove that their acceptance of him is not genuine. For such a member it is especially important that the group try to understand him from his point of view. It is also important that the group maintain their goals and ways of working toward them. It is harmful for both him and the group if he is allowed to destroy completely the principles on which the members are developing a group. Both he and they need a dependable structure with limits accepted by all.

CONCLUSIONS

The great variation in the functioning of members is both a challenge and an opportunity. It is a challenge since it is so dynamic and so deeply impregnated with possibilities which may be either destructive or constructive. It is an opportunity because its very nature can result in the discovery of the true meaning of communication in love.

Becoming a Group Member

Many persons enter a new world in their first group experience. They have previously been in groups but not in those without the usual competitive and evaluative procedures.

The progressive steps in becoming a group member vary for each individual, since each brings to the experience a past uniquely his own. One important consideration directly related to the member's past is the character of his perceptions.[4] Changes in perception of the other members individually and the group as a whole precede each step in the becoming process.

IMPORTANCE OF PERCEPTION

The perceptions of members vary along a continuum, from the broad and open to the narrow and closed.[5] Research indicates that the open-minded members have a greater readiness to examine their feelings and apparently possess more insight into their personal needs.[6] The relatively closed-minded group members are more content-oriented and less introspective. They also tend to project their repressed feelings onto the group.

A gradual change takes place with each group meeting. Although the change flows in one direction for all, its characteristics and rate differ widely within the two groups. The open-minded relax more easily and gain a feeling of adequacy and belongingness earlier in the process. The more closed-minded feel a need for clarity and answers for a longer period of time. They also become involved more slowly, and proceed in self-understanding with greater difficulty.

The differences in perception noted between the two groups continue in the latter part of the experience. Each member moves along the process of becoming in a slightly different manner and at a different rate. The more open he is in his attitudes, the more easily the member becomes involved, feels comfortable, develops interest in other members and achieves some sense of responsibility.

The more closed the member is in his attitudes the greater the continuing difficulty he has with the natural ambiguity of group process. He accepts it only gradually. Insights concerning the group and himself come more slowly, since self-concern, fear, and insecurity inhibit them. Self-concern hinders him from putting into action his sense of responsibility, which develops slowly. This closed-minded member moves toward the same goals of becomingness as the open-minded member but at a slower rate.

STAGES IN BECOMING

The developmental process of becoming a group member arranges itself logically into three stages: an introductory or unfreezing stage, a moving stage, and a freezing stage. The stages are continuous and overlapping and keep repeating themselves with each new level of aspiration.

Each of the three stages has its own special characteristics. The *unfreezing stage* is characterized by: (*a*) wonderings and questionings about the group experiences; (*b*) tentative beginnings of involvement and some feeling of relaxation; (*c*) attempts to listen, a little more sense of adequacy, and less self-concern. The *moving stage* is characterized by: (*a*) becoming accustomed to ambiguity, and the lack of answers and intellectual certitude; (*b*) recognition of individual differences, commencement of a positive attitude toward conflict; (*c*) realization of the importance of skills and the growing intention to develop these. The third or *freezing stage* is characterized by: (*a*) growing appreciation of a knowledge of group process and interpersonal relationships; (b) increasing openness and willingness to be known, some feeling of adequacy and understanding of others; (*c*) a sense of growth in self-knowledge, increase in sensitivity, interest in the process, and recognition of the need of more experience to improve skills.

FIRST STEPS TOWARD SELF-RENEWAL

All members feel some uneasiness and inadequacy in the first session.[7] Each fears that he may be in a competitive situation in which his efforts may be unacceptable. His self-concern inhibits his cooperation with others.

He senses that the atmosphere of this group is different —more understanding and considerate than he expected. He begins to relax and listen because he realizes that there is no evaluation. He notices that the leader listens carefully to everyone, and he may recognize that he himself listens only to those whom he expects in advance to have ideas which are interesting and usable.

He is a little surprised that the leader is not taking a more active part. The discussion is progressing without the leader's direction, and he notices that the other members are not especially interested in or desirous of having the leader's support or encouragement. He begins to feel that it is his group and he gradually becomes involved. He ventures ideas and finds that members listen to his comments.

When he hears conflicting points of view expressed, he is impressed that creative differences are acceptable. He senses that genuineness is evidently the criterion. He becomes aware that the relationship among members is changing. He is becoming interested in others and in the progress of the group.

He recognizes that members are speaking spontaneously and enthusiastically without censoring their thoughts. Each member's personal statements are accepted as truth for him and are given consideration. He senses that he is no longer apprehensive when others commence talking about their personal problems. He recognizes that all members have weaknesses and strengths similar to his own. These, he notes, are accepted with understanding as part of the search for a better life for everyone.

He recognizes that he is able to listen and to function with some skill in reflection, clarification and analysis. He experiences a growing assurance that he is becoming more adequate. At times he may still find some difficulty in following the thread of thought and in mentally organizing the sequence of ideas. However, he helps to provide information and clarification on the issues discussed. This participation gives him feelings of usefulness and satisfaction. He is aware that he cares for the members in the group and feels some responsibility for their well-being and progress in the experience.

7 SPECIAL PROBLEMS IN INTERACTION

Size of Group

The ideal number of members in a group remains a moot question.[1] Group leaders disagree on the optimum size, since each leader judges the issue in terms of his own experience. Research, although lacking the validity and preciseness we may desire, has nevertheless been helpful in formulating useful guidelines for leaders.

One useful guide is that presented by Thelen, who has investigated the issue in terms of the "least group size." By this phrase he means that a group should have only the number of members necessary to serve the emotional needs of the group and to get the job done. The least possible number of members necessary to take care of these two needs is then considered the optimum size.

This principle provides a starting place. Its application, however, becomes difficult as the purposes, structures and skills of the members differ from group to group. Persons who are experienced members and have at their disposal various group skills are likely to have more satisfactory interaction in larger groups than those who are inexperienced.

Sometimes the minimum number for a group is set at two or three persons. A two-person group may be used in the initial stages of getting acquainted but three persons is a more useful and meaningful minimum for a group.

Uncertainty and disagreement also persist with reference to the maximum number of persons for a group. In general a maximum size for a group is hard to determine and varies under certain circumstances. Group sizes are generally arbitrarily chosen but are not too different from the following designation. A small group consists of 3-7 members, a medium group from 5-15 members and a large group over 15. Beyond twenty-five problems related to cohesiveness and interaction increase mathematically.

It is agreed by members and leaders alike that interaction, a sense of belonging and a feeling of acceptance become increasingly difficult as the group increases in size. In educational settings the general custom is to divide a large number into groups of three, six, nine, and eighteen, or a similar division. The membership commences in groups of three. After several meetings, depending upon the feelings of the members, groups of six are formed, and the process continues after a number of meetings, increasing the size. Some members adjust more easily to a larger group than others do. Secure individuals who feel generally adequate and are open to experience make the adjustment to a larger group without much difficulty. I am conducting a group at this time in which the members are discussing the change from groups of seven to a large group of twenty-one. Some express the doubt that the skills and attitudes which they have developed would transfer to the large group, saying, "Maybe we'll have to start all over again." They recognize that the large-group situation would require that they observe, listen to, and become sensitive to many more persons.

The size of the group in relation to its purposes should also be considered. If the aims of the group are educational, a large group of twenty may perform quite well. This is especially true if the interaction of the members can be given time to develop. A large group requires several meetings to gain the rapport and sense of cohesiveness which develops early in a small group of five or seven.

If the aims of the group are the discussion of personal problems and concerns, a smaller group of five to seven is desirable. A small group makes more possible the development of trust in one another. It also encourages a willingness to become more personally involved.

The optimum size of the group is related to the experience of the leader. A beginning leader could be expected to perform better in a small group. In a large group more demands are placed on the leader. He observes more people, listens to more ideas, offers more clarifications and reflections. The situation requires that he relate to and try to understand more persons than the leader of a small group. Relating to five or seven members is much less demanding than relating to fifteen or twenty persons.

From the viewpoint of the members a small group provides many more satisfactions than a large group. Research done by James Schellenberg in an academic college setting indicated that those in small groups of four to ten members received more satisfaction from a semester's experience than did those in large groups. When members are asked to describe the nature of their satisfactions, they respond that they get to know one another better in small groups and that they feel accepted and "can say anything they want to."

Sometimes it is difficult to have groups of the preferred size. Leaders find that results are much more satisfactory if a large group is divided into two small groups, and the leader meets alternately with each small group, even though it means dividing the total time between the two groups.

Occasionally a leader may unexpectedly be confronted by, for example, sixty people who desire to participate in the discussion of a timely topic relevant to their lives. He is forced to decide among several possibilities:

1. He may consider a brief lecture to the total group

followed by discussion in small groups of five to ten persons. Discussion in small groups would be followed by reports from each group to the total group. This method, however, depends upon the number of those present who might be able to serve as leaders of the small groups.

2. He may divide the group into four sections of approximately fifteen persons each and arrange different periods in order that he may meet with each group. This demands much more of his time but permits the development of a true group experience for all.

3. If a very large room or several adjoining rooms are available he may decide first to divide the total enrollment into two parts, A and B, each with approximately thirty persons. Groups A and B would then be subdivided into small groups of five, six, or ten persons. Each small group would have a rotating leader and observer for each meeting. The leader of each small group would meet with the leader of the total group in advance to discuss the content and process in his group. The leader would rotate among the small and large groups in each meeting of two to three hours. The large groups, A and B, would meet each evening in their small groups and also in the large group. For example Group A might meet in small groups for forty-five minutes followed by a fifteen-minute break, and then in the large group for forty-five to sixty minutes. In the large group, reports would be heard regarding the key ideas discussed in the small groups and these would be followed by further discussion.

4. In the group of sixty persons the leader may find that all are unfamiliar with group process and none has had sufficient experience to function as a leader of a small group. He may be unwilling to use small groups, and may consider instead dividing the total group into A and B (approximately thirty persons in each). He would then divide his

time, spending one-half of the meeting time with A and the other half with B. In this case, for example, Group A may commence at 7:00 P.M. and Group B at 8:30 P.M., assuming this is an evening meeting.

The leader may also consider using the following arrangement with the plan described above. He may meet with half the group, with fifteen persons seated in a circle and the remaining fifteen seated in an outer circle, but close to the inner circle in order to be able to hear and observe. After about forty-five minutes, and a break of ten to fifteen minutes, the persons in the two circles reverse positions and the discussion continues.

In trying to decide which arrangements he will use, the leader has several factors to consider: (1) How important is it that the members have a true or organic group experience and not just a discussion group? (2) How important is it that the leader conduct the groups personally? (3) Does the leader have among the enrolled members persons trained in group process who could lead small groups, or could he secure such persons?

Regardless of which choice he makes, the leader will plan to have regular and frequent evaluations of the process in which the members are engaged.

As the group increases in size it becomes evident that there is a decrease in the opportunity for individual verbal interaction (more people are likely to be silent), for learning the skills of group process and for increasing one's self-understanding and understanding of others. More groups are necessary as numbers increase if the quality of the group experience is to be maintained. This means the expenditure of more time and energy on the part of the leader. Leaders agree that it is better to have a quality experience for a small number rather than a mediocre experience for many.

Since the quality of the group experience bears a direct relation to the number of members in the group, some leaders consider that members themselves should participate in determining the group size and the necessary arrangements which follow. Such cooperative decisions made at the time of the formation of the group have been found to result in an earlier cohesiveness among the members who engage in making the decision.

The Silent Period

Leaders and members in many groups are uneasy when a period of silence develops.[2] They are uneasy for several reasons: (1) they are accustomed to equate verbal activity with progress in their interaction; (2) they find it difficult to believe that anything important is taking place during the silence; and (3) they assume that the total value of group process lies in the result.

The silent period needs to be examined from various perspectives. Recognition of the silence and discussion about it could help members to accept it as a normal group experience early in the group's development. This would be an improvement compared with the late acceptance which often occurs in the life of the group and tends to slow down its progress.

Silence in the group may mean many things, some positive and some of dubious usefulness. A prolonged silence may mean that the ideas presented are not clear. It may also mean that there are several dangling comments which are unrelated and the group is groping for a sense of direction. Both of these situations can be remedied by the members or the leader through clarifying and linking these ideas to show their relationship.

A silence may indicate that the members feel that they

are unable to contribute. This is likely to occur if the members perceive that knowledgeable and well-organized responses are expected. This is even more likely to occur when the leader or others frequently evaluate one another's responses. This should change as they become more accepting of one another and if the leader encourages this acceptance. He may do this through careful listening and nonevaluative reactions.

For some members silence indicates some degree of fear of becoming verbally involved. This fear may stem from many sources. It may be fear arising from the newness of the situation or from an inability to believe what they are experiencing—especially the unconditional acceptance of the members and leader. It may also be fear of the developing closeness and warmth of the interpersonal relationships. These members may feel that others will not like them when they really come to know them. It may be a fear of being unable to reciprocate properly the genuine caring of others.

For others it may be that silence denotes an assumed or real boredom. This boredom may result from an incongruence between their expectancies and what they perceive is happening in the group. Some members may expect many highly informative ideas to be expressed. They may be bored by the group's interest in the process and the developing interpersonal relationships. Silence may take place as a means of withdrawal from the situation. Other members who have had a good experience in another group may be looking for the same experience in this one. When they perceive that it is not taking place, they may also become bored and silent.

However, silence can be a sign of group progress and individual growth. During this time members may be balancing the turn of the group discussion with their own experiences and observations. They can deliberate without being whisked to another idea too abruptly. Silence is helpful to those who have difficulty in formulating their ideas in time to present them in a fast-flowing discussion. Silence, then, can be helpful to those who need time to develop their ideas. It is possible that they may then contribute them to the group. Even if these ideas go unspoken, each member clarifies his thinking and feeling. Such clarification increases the eventual possibility for a core of agreement in the thinking of the members and this core may become the basis for mutual understanding.

Careful, unhurried, reflective thinking also increases opportunity for considering both sides of a situation or for all pertinent aspects of a problem to come into focus and evaluation. This leads to greater understanding, to a more complete rapport and more effective three-way cooperation.

The experience of silence has value even though an idea may remain unexpressed. The opportunity which silence presents encourages the critical examination of others' ideas in relation to one's own. In this manner, the idea is placed in proper perspective and may one day appear in action.

Involvement

We agree that personal growth does not take place without involvement. How frequently we hear, "Now that I have thought it over, I have changed my mind." We also hear, "Now that we have discussed it, I feel much better." Involvement can be with oneself or with others, and nonverbal as well as verbal. We disagree on what kind and how much involvement is needed to induce behavioral change.

The degree of involvement among members is influenced by the amount of resistance each experiences. Participation in the group has a risk which results in feelings of ambivalence, hesitancy, overstatement, understatement and silence. All of us experience one or more of these forms of resistance to some degree. Leaders may need to help members to distinguish between resistance which prevents one from understanding and resistance which takes the form of rationalization for disregarding insight.

Resistance[3] in group members may appear at any stage in the life of the group. It is felt by the group as an influence which (*a*) hinders or disturbs the developing unity and rapport; (*b*) impedes the achievement of insight, especially with reference to the "here and now" problems of the group; and (*c*) obstructs the developmental changes in the process occurring within themselves and others in the group. Resistance may take two forms: resistance to insight and resistance to behavioral change after the insight is attained. Members can be helped to use productive imagination to diminish or eliminate their underlying fears. The group will eventually perceive that fear of change is basic to various forms of resistance. The leader hopes to develop a psychological climate in which resistance is accepted and understood and the fear of change reduced.

At one time we thought it sufficient to appeal only to reason. If the undertaking was reasonable, it was assumed that it would be accepted and acted upon. It was expected that emotions would be controlled by reason and suppressed if they opposed the dictates of reason. The will was relied upon for effecting decisions.

How the will functions has been a matter of controversy down to the present day. Since the time of Luther and Erasmus two viewpoints concerning the freedom and the bondage of the will have prevailed. Luther concluded that the will was in bondage. That is, he believed that, as part of the self, the will was subject to the internal change in the self in exercising its influence. Erasmus concluded that the will was free. His position was that although the will is part of the self, it is free and able to control its impulses.

Those who hold the Renaissance viewpoint of Erasmus assume that involvement results from a clear and definite appeal to reason in accord with the values of the person(s). The Reformation viewpoint expressed by Luther has become a strong rival and much criticism has been directed against the assumption that behavioral change will result from an appeal to reason. Those who favor the Reformation viewpoint consider it necessary to involve the whole person.

These two contrasting viewpoints have resulted in two very different methods of inducing involvement by individual persons and by groups. The Renaissance view has resulted in the use of the lecture as a chief means of involvement. Learning is viewed as the introjection of ideas of authorities who select what is important from the past. The Reformation view has resulted in the use of various methods such as debate, discussion and group process for the purpose of involving the whole person on the thinking, feeling, and acting levels.

The need for total involvement in order to induce behavioral change has been emphasized by several psychologists. Kurt Lewin has significantly influenced the thinking of the last two decades. His position is that genuine change does not take place unless the person becomes totally involved—in thinking, feeling, and acting.

More recently, researchers in motivation have concluded that emotion plays an important part in all types of behavior including decision-making. This has led to a change in attitude and methods in situations where change is hoped for. In many instances emotion has been elevated to the place of prime importance once held by reason.

A third significant influence came through the development and use of self-theory by Carl Rogers. This theory, which was a composite of several viewpoints including those of Kurt Lewin, ushered in a unique view of the conditions conducive to involvement and behavioral change. It uses the paradoxical idea of Lewin that genuine change takes place when a person is free not to change. It also initiated a new form of interpersonal relationships. It was assumed that unconditional acceptance and permissiveness to be what you really are would increase the possibility of involvement and change.

In this situation the person ceases to perform as he perceives an authority figure (group leader, counselor, employer, etc.) wants him to, and instead commences to examine his own position, values and goals. Having done so, he probably will set up his own personal goals and aspirations and move toward their attainment.

It is now generally accepted that the total involvement of the person is necessary for genuine change to take place. It is also assumed that the will[4] functions in relation to the desire for change of the total organism and that another part of us is more influential than the will. This has been called *intentionality.* Intentionality is the expression of what we really are. Involvement is significantly affected when our intentionality is not in accord with our will. We may carry out the prompting of our intentionality even in contradiction to what we will. As the apostle Paul said, "The things I would not, I do." Emotion is now recognized to be an integral part of all we do. The seeming use of emotion in decision-making without a similar emphasis on rational thought has led to much concern recently. It has also resulted in questionable and sometimes destructive group action.

Differences arise regarding the most effective method for making use of these insights. Some believe that members will not involve themselves unless there is the application of considerable psychological pressure. They increase this pressure through the use of ambiguity, frustration and interpretation. They also believe that the route to involvement is chiefly via the emotions. They assume that the intentionality of persons is to relate to others. They consider that normal resistance must and can be overcome by the increase of psychological pressure. These assumptions are basic to the T group, encounter group and sensitivity group.

Others disagree with this assumption. They believe that members involve themselves to the degree that they are encouraged to feel safe, adequate and accepted as they are. They trust this psychological climate to induce members to understand themselves through interaction and introspection. They also assume that, having done so, members will set useful, constructive goals and will move toward their achievement through interaction with others. They assume that the "rationality of the organism" or the intentionality is dependable in the person's becoming. These are the assumptions of the group-centered groups.

Each person in any group responds differently to the method used. Therefore no method is of optimum value for all. Those who have not developed their depth potential involve themselves differently from those who have.

Members also differ in the degree of their involvement, since each member involves himself according to his needs. These in turn influence his perception of the situation. Members satisfy their needs by both verbal and nonverbal participation. All of us use both methods.

All group leaders depend on involvement of the members for groupness to develop and change to take place. The methods each uses to secure involvement depend upon one's beliefs regarding how behavioral change takes place. Members differ widely in what causes them to become involved. Some members appear to need some kind of psychological pressure in order to become more than casually involved. Others need a different set of conditions. The ideal situation is a product of the "climate" of the group and the methods of the leader. These are expected to induce a normal and necessary amount of involvement for interest to develop and personal growth to take place.

Conflict

Formerly conflict[5] was believed to be only a sign of loss of control, of ineptitude, of lack of ingenuity. Today it is seen as being also useful and acceptable. It is considered a possible outcome of interpersonal acceptance and genuineness. There is recognition of the fact that we must be able to accept and use conflict constructively.

However, conflict may be destructive as well as constructive. It depends on how it is used, and this is our current problem—to learn how to use conflict creatively. One may experience conflict within himself and/or he may experience it in his relations with others. Conflict contains within it the possibility of one's emergence from it as a person with greater self-knowledge and purpose. Belief in the therapeutic value of conflict causes some to be dissatisfied unless it is overt. It is unfortunate that some people engender conflict for its own sake. These misunderstand the nature of genuine conflict and its usefulness to the persons involved.

NEEDED—A NEW PERSPECTIVE

The understanding of conflict requires a fresh, incisive look. Constructive conflict is indicative of the fact that: (*a*) members have accepted their interdependence; otherwise conflict would not arise; (*b*) they care about one another;

often group members who have great creative differences share a very deep relationship; (*c*) members have different needs and values, differences that become evident and produce conflict.

But these same qualities are the necessary ingredients for growth-producing discussion. How these potentials are used determines the outcome. In the past members have often evaded conflict. They may repress their individual differences and assign the direction of the group to an authority figure. Or they may not accept their differences and be taken over by such a leader. They may evade conflict by not facing up to the true reasons for its existence. More serious still, the members may resort to innocuous pleasantries in the actual presence of conflict feelings and hidden agendas.

What members do about conflict varies in relation to their learned patterns of dealing with it. Its usefulness in changing behavior is directly dependent upon the depth at which the members consider it. A conflict-producing topic in one group may lead to a deeper understanding of life and its meaning, but the same topic in another group may result in ways of eliminating the apparent cause of conflict and of avoiding it in the future. The usefulness of conflict in deepening and enriching the members' personal lives bears a direct relation to the depth at which members are willing and able to consider their differences.

PROBLEMS WITH CONFLICT

Some people seem to thrive on conflict. For them nothing important in the group happens without it. Unless there is conflict they are uneasy and feel the whole endeavor lacks purpose. Conflict may satisfy their drives for identity, a sense of adequacy, or power. They overparticipate but are not changed. They appear to lack a commitment to the members of the group. Without conflict they cannot allow themselves to be influenced by ideas and attitudes different from their own.

Others enjoy conflict for its own sake. They are seized by its seeming vitality, since it affords them a means of releasing frustrations, escaping from boredom or of avoiding demanding responsibilities.

Some people know only conflict. They have not developed the level of organizational ability necessary to perceiving ways in which they could sublimate their negative impulses through constructive channeling. Lacking impulse control they may be caught up in imitative and destructive behavior. Leaders experience much difficulty in helping them to become interested in cooperative behavior and in aiding them to develop a sense of responsibility.

Still others may have these or other difficulties but they avoid conflict. This occurs sometimes when the topic of the group focuses directly on a similar conflict in their personal lives. This is especially true if they have suppressed it and are now reluctant to discuss it, or it may be that they have resigned themselves to believing that not much can be done. Their general attitude is to adjust and not to expect too much. This position frees them from recognizing their obligation for decision-making and taking responsibility. Apathy is a ready-made excuse for not becoming involved. They have no heart for "going against the tide." They do not deepen their lives or espouse their human dignity. They are content to live only with "the courage to be as a part."

THE CREATIVE HANDLING OF CONFLICT

Conflict can reduce us to our lowest denominator. It tends to blot out from our awareness everything not relevant to our self-defense. If we succumb to our lesser selves, we may not handle the conflict creatively. In fact we may do one of the following: We may rise to the bait of insult—and this is a key failure. Or we may defend ourselves either by fight or by flight. If we can avoid these pitfalls we may handle the situation constructively.

If we do not allow our vision to be constricted we tend to keep our equilibrium in a broader framework than the angry "here and now." As a next step we resist seeing others as Willful Aggression and ourselves as Righteous Indignation. We then may be able to see ourselves and others as human beings. We grant to others and ourselves the same basic qualities. Then all may realize their capability of reappraising the relationship.

It may now be possible for us to express to one another our doubt, wonders and perplexities. When they are honest, such expressions have a way of inducing a sense of species, an "all in the same boat" feeling. Regardless of how different our backgrounds may be, we are at one in the experience of living in a baffling universe, uncertain of which way to turn.

In all these relationships each partner to the conflict has retained his human dignity. Each is related to the other in a person-to-person, or I-Thou relationship.

There are then certain conditions which must prevail if we are to handle conflict creatively. We must not succumb to fight or flight. We must keep alive within ourselves a broader sense of reality than the conflict induces, and we must see one another as fellow human beings. Each of us must acknowledge his own doubts and fears. Each must credit the other with the willingness and ability to contribute ideas and insights.

Thus it is evident that the creative handling of conflict is not easy. Much depends on the personality and being of those who find themselves in conflict. The person challenged by hostility who does not hit back has worked out his own inner conflicts to the degree that he is relatively at peace with himself. Such members in a group are able to see beyond the threatening present and respond adaptively and flexibly. They recognize the inadequacy of things as they are but also feel that something can be done.

They are not driven to act impulsively and are able to exercise their human prerogative to think it over. They can wait. They display the type of courage which is possessed by the person who is not fighting himself. They have deep wells of emotional resources and can therefore risk rejection, or attack or being made to look ridiculous. They trust their own resilience, their powers of "comeback."

They can be patient. They sense that their patience must be commensurate with the complexity of the problem. Their patience is not that of the arrogant self-righteous who say, "Well now, it's up to them." Nor is it that of one who settles down to tolerate what is intolerable. Nor is it the patience of the self-appointed martyr who asks to be affronted in order to have the chance to feel sorry for himself and sorry for the challengers. Instead it is the patience of the person with a deep sense of meaning and commitment to life, one who has a vital sense of the failure without feeling that he has failed.

Group process can nurture the view of conflict as a transitional stage in becoming truly human. Each member can be helped to deepen his life, to accept his human dignity and to meet the demands of "going against the tide" when the situation calls for it.

Improvement in Group Functioning

Improvement in group functioning is unlikely to take place by chance. It comes about through planned progress,[6] as the result of ongoing evaluation and the use of the insights obtained in this manner. Evaluation may take place during the process, at the close of each meeting, or at both times. This is made easier if the group members in turn act in the capacity of observer for one or more meetings. Members find this function a helpful one to them in their own development and that of the group.

The observer needs criteria to guide his observations. In order to provide these, the group develops guidelines which they consider would help them to become a "good" group. One criterion of a good group is that it accomplish what it sets out to do. The problem becomes one of examining the steps the group should take to reach its production goal efficiently and to determine the stages of group growth leading toward efficient group production.

A second criterion revolves around the degree to which the group's immediate goals relate themselves to the broader goals of society. Are the goals of the group and the methods used to attain them transferable to society and in keeping with its goals?

A third criterion is how responsible the members become in helping one another to grow toward increasingly efficient group functioning. A good group utilizes its member-potential in the achievement of its goals.

A fourth criterion is how well this group is "growing" its members, how well it is helping them to understand themselves and others that they may become even better contributors.

In summary, then, a "good" group is one which encourages efficient group functioning, relates its functioning to social goals, utilizes its member-potential and promotes member-growth.

How does the observer proceed to use these criteria? His function is to stimulate the group to assess its degree and rate of progress in the areas of (1) efficient group functioning; (2) awareness of broader social goals; (3) full member-utilization; and (4) promotion of member-growth. Accordingly, he makes observations pertinent to the four areas and focuses the members' attention on their functioning in these areas. He will try to do this in a way which will enable the members to use his observations to understand the process and their own interaction in order to improve their functioning.

To be most useful, the observer has to decide what levels of functioning he will use in relation to the group in which he is member. He functions on two general levels: the calling-to-attention or descriptive level and the why-did-it-happen or interpretative level. The descriptive level is in actuality a selective playback. In his selection of what to report, the observer focuses the attention of the group on specific points or happenings. He hopes to encourage group and individual evaluation and decision on specific group problems. He may present such feedback as, "We were not able to reach any decision although we discussed two problems which required decision-making," or "We started right off today with several responses and much interaction."

Descriptive feedback is useful if it is a single committee meeting, or a one-day workshop or weekend conference. Such feedback will gradually give place to possible ideas concerning interaction as the group becomes more at ease and more cohesive.

The second level of observer-functioning is comprised of several procedures. The observer advances hypotheses or makes interpretations regarding the reasons for certain events. He adapts his remarks to the stage in which he perceives the group to be functioning. If the group is meeting regularly he may gradually increase the depth of his interpretations. Of course the sensitivity of the group to its problems and the degree of group objectivity present should guide the observer in making interpretations. How helpful the feedback is to the group varies from observer to observer, depending upon his understanding of the group process, the members themselves, and his own beliefs regarding what is useful.

All the members and the leader have a responsibility in providing feedback to one another. The observer has a special and greater responsibility in this area, since he accepts this function as his chief contribution. He is likely to have more pertinent observational material than any other member, since this is the focus of his effort.

The observer's functioning is more useful and acceptable if (1) he is viewed as a member of the group; (2) he has a high degree of sensitivity concerning his responsibility to make helpful contributions; and (3) he increasingly involves the members in making observations to free them from any dependence on his specialized function.

To fulfill his responsibilities in the manner suggested he must believe in the worth and effectiveness of the ongoing method of group process, in the possibility of the continuing growth of the members, and in sharing with them his function as observer as much as possible.

He will also strive to improve his skills. A primary skill is the capacity to distinguish between his own ideas, perceptions and feelings and those which actually exist. He cannot always be completely objective but he can learn to base his conclusions on specific and objective observations. To do this he records what happens. By doing this he can check his comments later against what actually took place. His efforts to develop this skill will induce him to become as sensitive as possible to a widening range of clues, which in turn provide more pertinent material for the group to consider.

The observer must decide the kinds of things he will observe, since he cannot observe everything. This will depend at least in part on the level of observation employed. If he is observing on the descriptive level he may observe such things as group atmosphere, cohesion, leader behavior, member roles and procedures for group process.

In any one session he will focus on what seems to be the special problem, event, or focus-of-interest of the group for that meeting. Sometimes the members themselves indicate what they would like the observer to consider.

The group may seem to be continuing too long as a collection of individuals rather than becoming a cohesive group. In this case he will observe such dimensions as atmosphere, cohesion, communication, and leader behavior. If the group is using a rotating-chairman system, it will be helpful to give some attention to leader behavior. If only a few of the members are improving their ways of responding, the observer may wish to point out ways in which members have and have not functioned.

As the group becomes familiar with the possible kinds of feedback it may ask the observer to observe and report on certain ways in which it hopes to improve. What to observe and feed back should be increasingly the decision of the group. If the group requests interpretations of the interaction which the observer feels may not be helpful, this becomes a matter for discussion and decision by everyone.

The most difficult decisions focus on what the interpretational range of observation should be; and when, how and to what degree interpretation should be used. What the observer will do depends on several factors. He must consider the degree to which his interpretation will be congruent with the mode of behavior and the expectancy of group members. He may decide not to use it or use it only to a limited degree.

The observer must also consider the current developmental stage of the group, that is, the maturity of the group members and the length of time the group has been meeting. This is especially necessary if he is to make any interpretations. His observations, for instance, will differ in relation to a kindergarten group, a group of high school students or an adult education group. He does not expect the same functioning of a group that has come together for a second meeting as he does of one which has been meeting regularly for six months. Also he makes allowances for a group which has had authoritarian leaders for years and is now working with a democratic leader using group process.

Many observers do not make interpretations themselves. They involve the members in evaluating the process. They may ask, "What did we do which helped us?" or "What can we do next time to improve?" Sometimes—especially in the beginning—the observer may ask the members to write their responses on cards, anonymously. The observer then feeds back the information to the entire group. It is preferable to have the group itself evaluate how well it is functioning in the various dimensions and to attempt some self-diagnosis of the reasons why it has or has not progressed in the different areas.

The group improves its functioning through development in several areas, namely, skills, decision-making and attitudinal changes. Some indications of development in skills are increased ability for concentration and listening, for clarification, reflection, synthesis, and the giving of information. Indications of improvement in decision-making are openness to conflicting points of view, ability to consider alternatives, ability to accept group decisions when not fully in accord with one's own. Indications of progress in attitudinal changes are acceptance of ambiguity, increase in openness, interest in others, spontaneity. Further indications are the increase of reality-testing among members, the nature and degree of involvement of the members, understanding of and ability to use conflict constructively.

Evaluation through the use of an observer is one means of improving the group's function. Regular and planned evaluation of the group process is one of the primary requirements if progress is to take place.

8 *PUTTING GROUP PROCESS TO WORK*

In Conferences

A conference[1] is a demanding test of the use of group process. Its very nature makes necessary careful planning and realistic goals. Difficulties focus on brevity, numbers and unfamiliarity of the participants with one another and with group process.

Most conferences are brief, one session, one day, a day and an evening, two days, or perhaps three. Beyond that they are generally considered workshops. The longer the time the participants spend together the more can be accomplished. Brevity, then, imposes limitations and goals must accommodate themselves to what is realistic.

ESSENTIALS

Regardless of their brevity certain experiences are necessary if the use of group process is to succeed. Opportunity must be provided for the conferees to get to know something of one another as a prerequisite to cooperative planning. Then a goal must be established which can be accomplished without pressure but within the time limit. Highly skilled leadership is a necessity especially when time is short. There is a need to consider the degree to which formulated plans have a chance of succeeding; lastly, a careful evaluation is needed of what was helpful and how improvement could be made if a similar session were to be undertaken later.

The shorter the time the more likely that the experience

will be one of group discussion only rather than of group process. In group discussion the competitive atmosphere and evaluative procedures exist. Members do not have the experience of relating to one another as persons. They do not feel that they understand themselves or others any differently from when the conference began. This is the kind of situation to avoid. The goal of those planning and conducting the conference should be to change the experience from the familiar one of group discussion to the unfamiliar one of group process.

NECESSARY DECISIONS

However, this is difficult to do. The following will assist in making group process become a reality. If there is a program or an announcement of the event, mention that small groups will be used. Indicate on the program when small groups will be used and the topic or purpose of each small-group meeting. If the nature of the conference is exploratory it may be useful to mention that the purpose and topic of discussion will be decided in each small group. Such procedures will help the conferees to get used to the idea of participating in small groups before the actual experience.

One of the first decisions to be made by the members of the program planning committee is that of the general purpose of the conference. Is the chief purpose of the conference instructional; to discuss policy and program to be used in members' units at home; to decide regarding a plan, a program or a structure; to learn of group process and its possibilities for use in their organization; or to provide an experience for each to improve in interpersonal communication and to grow in self-understanding and understanding of others?

A second consideration for the committee is how much

structure to build into the conference. In this area they should consider such ideas as: Shall we have someone to present information or inspiration or both as a means of stimulating the conferees and clarifying the issues to be discussed? What proportion of the time will be spent in small groups? How will these small groups be organized? Will the conference be open or invitational? If invitational shall an invitation be extended to those with a variety of backgrounds and interests or to those of similar backgrounds and interests? How definitively will the program be planned? Will a set time be allotted to each activity?

A third area of responsibility is that of leadership. What leaders are available who are trained in the kind of small-group process desired? Who would coordinate and plan with these leaders of small groups? When, where and how many times will the coordinator of the leaders and the leaders of small groups meet? In each small group for how many will the leaders be responsible? It should be noted that the number of participants at the conference should bear a direct relationship to the number of small-group leaders available. Planning should be made for other needed leaders or experts. Then, do these experts favor the use of small groups and will they be comfortable with the format of the conference as planned by the committee?

A fourth consideration is a suitable location for the conference. One primary consideration is space and sufficient movable chairs, preferably tablet chairs. Adequate space does a great deal toward the success of the conference. If one room will not accommodate all the small groups, additional rooms used should be adjacent to one another.

A fifth concern is what form of report on the conference will be most useful to the participants. How will this be compiled and who will be responsible for it? The report should include comments on the ways in which interpersonal communication developed as well as ideas related to the general topic of the conference itself. A useful and interesting part of the conference report will contain quotes from anonymous self-reports on the conference, the feelings of the members, the aspects of the conference which were most worthwhile, and those which could be improved.

WORKABLE PLANS

The kind of planning necessary for a group is determined by the number of participants expected. If a large number attends, more structure may be necessary to ensure that each has a good group experience. When the number exceeds fifty, the use of several experienced group leaders becomes a necessity. Preconference meetings of all the leaders to work out aims and procedures are exceedingly important. These leaders are an important influence in the encouragement of an accepting and nonevaluative climate and procedures.

It is assumed at a conference that there are certain ideas, plans, problems or procedures which will need consideration by all participants. Some committees plan to present this kind of input through an address or lecture designed for this purpose and given by an authority in the area. If this method of input is used, the committee must plan definite ways in which the ideas of the lecture will be challenged, examined, changed, and added to in small groups.

Some planning committees do not use a speaker as a source of input. They assume that those attending the conference are versed to a degree in the problems, plans and ideas of the large organization and their local units. In this case it is well if the group leaders reach a consensus in advance with reference to the issues, plans and ideas they will incorporate in their discussions. It may be well to plan to have resource persons who supply information as required by any group when such is sought.

Other planning committees use a third method. Instead of deciding in advance the general aims of the conference and what should be discussed, they invite to a planning conference representatives who assist in planning both the content and the procedures to be used. Such representatives should be invited well in advance. This gives them a chance to discuss what they think would be most useful with members of the local organization. This kind of planning has the best chance of meeting the needs of those who attend.

These same representatives should be invited to participate in the evaluation of the usefulness of the conference. To be able to do this they must engage in planning the criteria for deciding what information is needed and the means of securing it.

Among the important procedures which need discussion by the committee and group leaders is the use of observers in the small groups. The committee will decide the process of selection, the observers' function and the presentation of their observations. The remarks of the observers together with those of the members and leader are usually very useful. They can emphasize what makes for helpful group process and can also recognize the quality of their own attitudes and procedures.

Sometimes a committee has to work with far less than an ideal situation. For instance in one conference the planning committee for a conference of 150 persons found it possible to have only one experienced leader in group process and five other group leaders with minimal experience. The chief problems were to assist the leaders with minimal experience to be useful and helpful in their groups and how to have group process with so few leaders.

The first problem was minimized by meetings of the experienced leader and the five group leaders. Together they carefully thought through the situation, trying to foresee difficulties which could arise, to understand how best they could function and what goals they could expect to accomplish.

The second problem—the number of persons in each small group—required much thought. The leaders were skeptical concerning the amount and quality of the interaction if the groups were large. They finally arrived at the idea of dividing the participants into five groups of thirty each, with one leader to each group. Then it was planned to spend twenty minutes in groups of three to get acquainted and to discuss generally the topic of the conference.

Each large group of thirty would then be divided into two groups of fifteen each with approximately the same number of men and women in each group. The two subgroups of fifteen each formed themselves into two concentric circles. One group of fifteen comprised the inner circle and the second group of fifteen the outer circle. The inner circle, with the leader, engaged in discussion. Those in the outer circle listened and observed, and helped in the evaluation of the process going on in the inner circle.

For the second period of discussion the two circles reversed positions. Since each group observed and listened to the other there was no interruption in the direction of the discussion.

One representative from each group of fifteen brought back reports, questions and concerns to the total group. For this part of the conference the 150 conferees were arranged in four circles. The innermost circle was composed of the ten representatives from the subgroups, the five leaders of these groups and the experienced leader. The second circle included thirty-five conferees on slightly raised seats. The third circle consisted of forty-five persons on a circular platform raised above the level of the second circle. In the fourth (outside) circle were sixty persons on a circular platform raised just above level 3. Elevated seating made it possible for all to see and hear the discussion among the participants in the inner circle.

If necessary, the same design, but without raised seating, can be used with good results. It is important, however, that the chairs in circles 2, 3, and 4 are arranged in such a fashion that each person can see those in the inner circle. Each circle of chairs should be as close as possible to the preceding one in order that the remarks in the innermost circle can be heard by everyone.

Another committee planning a conference for 150 participants divided the total number into four groups of approximately thirty-five to thirty-eight persons in each. The conference provided four kinds of experience: lecture, movie, sociodrama and group process in small groups. The persons were divided into groups randomly at the time of registration by the color of the name card received. The program indicated the order and time of each experience for each group. The four experiences were integrated around the conference theme and the group discussion focused on the experiences in which members had just been involved.

This arrangement allowed for small groups of seven or eight persons with a leader for each group. Groups of this size made possible meaningful interaction and a sense of groupness. Since each small group met twice with each leader, a warmth and acceptance was experienced which added an important dimension for each participant.

CONCLUSIONS

There are, then, certain precautions each planning committee should take regarding the use of group process. Its use should conform to the purposes of the conference. The committee should not plan to use group process just for the purpose of using it. The groups should be small enough in size for good interaction to take place. The size should be partly determined by the purpose of the groups. Problem-solving groups concerned with specific problems and those desiring to discuss life-adjustment problems will accomplish their aims better if they have five or seven members rather than ten or fifteen. Those discussing organizational plans, educational ideas or general growth and development problems can accommodate ten to fifteen persons successfully.

The committee should plan for a leader with each small group. If possible these should be trained leaders with some experience. In any case, there should be a trained, experienced leader to work with the members of the planning committee. He should assist in the planning and conduct preconference meetings with the leaders of the small groups. Definite plans should be made to help the participants in the small groups to understand and learn group process. They should also be helped to become familiar with the criteria to use in evaluating process quality.

The use of group process does not ensure a successful conference. It is one way of minimizing the impersonality and superficiality that may exist in large groups. Group process can encourage a sense of adequacy, of belongingness and of personhood. It helps to make possible the securing of alternatives in a situation and the best thinking related thereto. It lends strength to cooperative planning and democratic action and creates the possibility that each participant may become a real person again with a "place in the sun."

In Teaching

The learning which results from current teaching leaves much to be desired. Learning at all age levels has often been individual, competitive and chiefly intellectual. The possibilities of using group process are only beginning to be adequately explored. The many educational values which could result from developing its use have not been thoroughly understood.[2] Also teachers generally have not been trained to build and maintain effective learning groups.

THE ORGANIC GROUP

The cooperative group enhances individual learning; improves the mental health of each member and the group as a whole; provides experience in effective, healthy social membership with peers and adults; supplies opportunities in social leadership and organization; integrates the intellectual and emotional learnings; encourages the use of new understandings; and helps each member to develop such values as the acceptance of others, caring for others, concern for the rights of others and a sense of responsibility for assisting one another and the progress of the group as a whole.

Not all of these possibilities are realized by every group or every member, but to some degree all are attained by any true group using group process. What, then, are some of the beliefs and procedures which characterize the teacher using group process?

THE CLASS BECOMES A GROUP

The teacher sets the tone within which the class works and out of which the members emerge into a group. To do this the teacher must believe in cooperative interaction. He must see the members as capable of dealing with problems, making decisions and exercising sufficient self-control for carrying out plans. He may find it necessary to reorganize himself in order to have action belief in the members and the process.

To change the atmosphere of an authoritarian, competitive class into that of a cooperative, interactive group, the teacher must release the miseducative tensions which classes tend to build in students. One of these is trying to understand what the teacher wants rather than trying to understand himself. A second is becoming dependent upon the teacher for evaluation of his work and the reward for succeeding. A third is the fear of not being able to do well what the teacher requires. Fourth, the student may be anxious and fearful about self-exposure, especially if he has a low personal assessment of his abilities.

In introducing group process the teacher must be the cooperative understanding person that he is from the outset. He works according to cooperative, democratic principles from the very beginning. By his actions he shows the members that he believes in them and respects them as persons. He encourages them to express their sentiments or to share their ideas and experiences. He acknowledges individual and group beliefs and opinions and helps the members to appraise them critically. He works with the group as a group; he does not evaluate; he does not call upon members to respond. He accepts their comments and listens very carefully. The members come to feel secure, to belong, to feel wanted. This certainty of acceptance is learned from the member's experiences in the group. Each member gradually comes to understand that being accepted as one is, regardless of one's behavior, is the field condition. The teacher believes that such a condition helps everyone to release creatively more of his real self into the environment.

THE GROUP DEVELOPS

Members change as the group changes and in the same direction. The teacher helps them to make plans and carry them out as a group. He is alert to recognize as many opportunities as possible in which to engage the group in making decisions. He refuses to be a "policeman" or disciplinarian in the usual sense. He expects that some will have good inner controls and others will not. He helps them to evaluate their capability of exercising self-control and plans with them in terms of their differences in this particular ability. The results of their decisions are cooperatively evaluated. The teacher may ask: "What are some things we did which helped us to have a good learning experience?" and "What are some ways we could improve next time?" He places great importance on the development of inner control.

As they evaluate the process the members gradually develop a sense of responsibility toward the group and toward each other. They learn to appreciate one another as each member gradually becomes known to the others. They come to understand that learning is overall growth and that the atmosphere and one's feelings are important elements in the learning experience. Increasingly the members realize that there are many important ways of contributing to the group other than supplying information. The teacher emphasizes their growth as a group and the specific content learning equally. He is careful through this emphasis to help the members feel important and necessary on the basis of their helpfulness to the group as much as on the basis of facts learned and intellectual problem-solving.

Members act as observers and they and the teacher report on the progress of the group in terms of their growth as a group and the learning of skills. These are, for example, becoming more comfortable with silences; more concentrated listening; sharing of time, giving each one desiring to speak an opportunity; clarifying ideas for one another and summarizing.

WHAT OF THE BEGINNER?

There is a false assumption that teachers generally plan cooperatively with their students at all age levels. Though they may spend years in authoritarian homes and schools, it is expected that they will be democratic the moment they accept the responsibility of teaching.

The current expectation that teachers should plan democratically leads to pseudo-democracy. A teacher may say: "We planned to visit the museum today but we haven't much time and most of us are working on the new math problems. What do you think we should do?"

The children know that the teacher wants them to work on the problems and a few respond in compliance with his wishes. But the teacher may be aware of the pretense. If so, he knows that his gesture was unconvincing and this knowledge makes him feel threatened and weakens his chances of becoming genuinely democratic in his teaching approach.

The teacher moves slowly in his attempt to use group process. This is necessary, since he is engaged in two different kinds of becoming. The first and most important change he must make is that of becoming a democratic person. Second, he will need to develop skills in group process.

Each teacher proceeds at the rate that is comfortable. He recognizes that it is easier to be democratic in situations in which he feels secure than in those in which he feels insecure and to some degree threatened. He carefully considers each situation in advance. In trying to determine if he can be democratic using group process he uses the following questions as a guide: Will I be able to accept the thinking of the members, especially when they make decisions which are different from my own viewpoint? Are the members capable of dealing with this problem? Could they be expected to make a workable, constructive decision with their experience and knowledge? Would the administration or others who place confidence in me be willing for me to proceed as I am planning to do? Of these questions the first is the most important. Unless the teacher can give a strong, positive response to this one, he should not proceed further. In this way he will avoid becoming authoritarian at some point in the decision-making process.

Teachers often complain that they do not have the freedom to be democratic rather than confront the fact that they are not able to respect the members' thinking. This may be true in some instances but often it is the failure to recognize opportunities for planning cooperatively. How many of us would have seen an opportunity in the situation, below, that faced Mr. Smith?

At the opening of school Mr. Smith was told that his Grade 6 would be required to cover the program and take a test at the end of the term. Weeks later, he realized that although the members and he had been interested and busy, they were behind in preparation for the test. He explained the requirement and asked the students what they thought could be done.

They suggested that each one determine for himself how much he had to learn, estimate the amount of time he would need to learn it, and plan his time to work on it, accordingly. The teacher, they thought, could help each student if and when he needed it, and those who already knew most of the material could help others. The teacher who believes in and uses group process finds unexpected ways in which to involve students in cooperative planning.

The teacher should be genuine and should refrain from

playing a role. When he can be democratic and use cooperative group process he should do so. At other times he should perform in his usual way, doing the planning, making decisions and requiring that they be honored. The students usually understand. They recognize that when a situation is presented for discussion, the teacher is prepared to respect and accept their thinking. They participate because they know the situation is genuine. If possible the teacher should "level" with the students explaining that for the time being he is making the decision with regard to the matter under consideration.

The teacher improves gradually. He is encouraged by the results he obtains and feels more confident as he becomes more aware of his limitations. He finds he is able to accept students' ideas more comfortably even when they are far from ideal and are (as he sees them) inferior to his own. He relies on regular evaluation of the process with the students as a means of improving it.

The teacher gradually learns how to help the students understand and use group process for satisfying their needs. He shows them how to work together on the activities which they cooperatively plan. The students gradually feel differently about him. They accept him as a friend, expert in helping them to resolve their needs while retaining their dignity and feeling of adequacy. The teacher focuses his services *to* them and not *on* them. They come to know and appreciate the meaning of interdependence.

CRITICAL INCIDENTS

In almost any group, leader and members may confront at least one critical incident which is an unusual conflict in interpersonal relationships having positive or negative results. This may take place even with experienced leaders. These incidents may be described as experiences in the life of the group which make a significant difference to its ongoingness. Generally they require an important decision by either leader or members, or by both.

Critical incidents are a test of the groupness of the group. They are a test of the teacher's flexibility in solving problems and his willingness to work with the members for outcomes satisfactory to all. At these times the students discover or rediscover how much the group experience means to them and their relationship with the other students in their group.

Mr. Jones taught history to Grade 8 students. He was interested in history and in the students. But he was dissatisfied with the lack of interest of some of the students, especially a small group of boys who were older than the others.

One day a boy in this group interrupted the class by exclaiming, "You are a rotten teacher!" The other students looked stunned and apprehensive. Another of the boys in this small group laughed. There was dead silence for what must have seemed to many a long time.

After Mr. Jones had regained his composure he said, "I know many of you are not interested and I, too, am dissatisfied with my teaching. If you recognize a rotten teacher maybe you would know a good teacher. Perhaps you can help me to become the good teacher I would like to be."

This incident could have resulted in a disaster for both teacher and students. Instead it was the beginning of a growing, interesting and valuable experience for all. Mr. Jones, because of his own security and genuineness, was able to place the conflict within a large framework, thus turning it into a cohesive rather than a divisive experience.

Miss Armstrong wondered what to do. The principal had sent a note stating that her fourth grade would have to give up going to the swimming pool unless they could go quietly. She knew that they were noisy but she had tried threats, punishments and rewards. None of them worked. She had read about working cooperatively with students but had not tried it.

She sat at her desk that afternoon thinking about it long after the children had gone. Something had to be done. Could she plan with the children? Would they have ideas and could she count on their carrying them out? Would the principal be in favor of using this planning method? She considered all these questions and decided to plan with the children what to do.

The next day she told them that she had received the note, explained the situation and asked them for suggestions. The children seemed amazed, unable to understand. Then one boy volunteered, "Why don't you make us behave? You're the teacher." Another said, "If someone is noisy send him back to the room." "You could make rules," said a third, "and send anyone who broke them to the principal."

Miss Armstrong could hardly believe the effect that years of conditioning had had on the children. After a pause she said, "You seem to think that this is my problem. I think it's ours."

There was a long silence. Then Mary volunteered, "Each of us could take care of himself."

"I don't think so," came swiftly from John. "Some of us may be able to but a lot of us can't."

Miss Armstrong responded: "It seems that some of us think we can take care of ourselves and others think we can't."

After another long silence, she continued, "Some of us know that we are strong enough to control ourselves, but perhaps others haven't tried, or have found that they are not strong enough. Suppose each one of us considers whether or not he is strong enough to take care of himself on the way to the pool. Each of you alone knows how he feels about it."

After a pause she asked, "Who of you think you are strong enough to control yourselves?" Many of the hands went up. "Are any not sure you can control yourselves?" Several hands went up. George said, "Those who can take care of themselves won't need any watching, and you can watch the others."

"You are making it my problem," Miss Armstrong said. "I think it is our problem. We'll plan together, but it is the problem of each of us and all of us together."

Another long silence. Then Jean said, "Why can't those of us who are strong help the others?"

"How could we do it?" asked Bill.

"Each of us could walk beside someone who wasn't sure," responded Fred. The children and Miss Armstrong accepted the plan.

As they walked quietly through the building, Miss Armstrong felt a new kind of freedom, a new feeling of adequacy in the group. Each one seemed filled with a new sense of self-respect as he demonstrated his ability to accept his obligation. Since the responsibility was individualized and shared, she herself relaxed.

A critical incident impels some teachers to try something new. Miss Armstrong would probably continue this cooperative planning as she and the children grew in the use of it. Teachers need to venture in the use of it in small ways before something critical forces a difficult situation and too great a risk.

What would happen and what would Miss Armstrong have done if the children had not controlled themselves? This is an unlikely possibility, especially because the students desired the outcome to be gained if they performed as agreed upon. However, in the event that the children could not be quiet, it would be hoped that Miss Armstrong would make it a group learning experience. The direct result would be that at least for the time being the students would lose their chance to go swimming.

If they found out for themselves that they were unable to go swimming, this would require a group discussion. The teacher would help them to recognize and accept the fact of their failure. In this manner they would learn that they succeed or fail as a group, that they are interdependent. Also they would plan for the future. When they felt they had progressed to a point that they could succeed, there would be another opportunity to try. They would be helped to realize that the amount of freedom they could have was directly related to the amount for which they could be responsible. Miss Armstrong would be alert to recognize opportunities she could provide to help them to develop their inner controls and thus become more able to be responsible.

WORKING WITH THE CULTURALLY DEPRIVED

"Culturally deprived" refers to people who have not benefited or have not had the opportunity to benefit from acceptable and constructive cultural conditioning. These persons may be found in any segment of society. They are found in proportionately larger numbers in the inner city. The culturally deprived have the following characteristics in varying degrees. They usually have a low level of impulse control and a weak memory trace; they are deficient in the use of both reactive and productive imagination and lack experience in discovering alternatives in a conflict situation.

The suburban child or adolescent is likely to rely more on his rational analysis and less on emotional discernment or the "wisdom of the organism." A teacher with a heterogeneous group of eight children in the sixth grade in a middle-class urban school also worked with a sixth-grade group in an urban inner-city school. Using a tape recorder each group recorded questions to which the other group responded. One question was, "What is your first wish?"

A boy in the first group (middle-class urban) said he would like to be a professional hockey player but he couldn't skate well enough. A boy in the second group (inner city) taped the response for him. "I think if you work hard enough, you could become a good hockey player but if I were you I would give my first choice to something more important."

An inner-city group of seventh-graders faced the situation in which one of their peers (not in their group) had marred a wall project on which they had worked. All of the ideas they developed as a means of handling the situation suggested some form of physical punishment. The same situation was presented to a middle-class group of seventh-graders in the same urban center but not in the inner city. They suggested these ideas: "Ask him if he really meant to do it or if it was an accident." "Bring everyone together and talk about it, because he may have been getting back at them for something one of them had done." "Ask him to put it back as it was; it could be that others will help him if he is really sorry." "Ask him to get a group to help him and fix it up by a certain time." "Bring him and the group working on the project together to get ideas for what do do, but not just to punish him."

The inner-city youth lacking both facility in expression and experience in thinking of alternatives have difficulty in thinking in terms other than force, punishment and conflict. Whereas those of the middle class apparently do not experience the frustration and conflictual feelings and can therefore think of other possibilities.

Most difficult for the teacher is to understand the ego

functioning of his students. "Ego" is defined as "that part of the personality which is engaged in keeping us in touch with reality and with helping us to regulate our impulse expression so that it is within the bounds which such a reality dictates." [3] If the decision presents a choice between right and wrong, there is further complication because of the relationship between conscience and ego and between both of these and the impulses.

Because of environmental influences, the culturally deprived have more frustrated and destructive emotions than suburban children. This is heightened further by their frequent failure in task challenges. As a result they find it difficult, or they are unable, to examine fear, anxiety or frustration without breakdown into impulsive, disorganized aggression. They do this instead of learning other ways of gratification which other youth and adults generally learn.

The teacher misses consistency of performance with this group. Many inner-city persons do not store up enough of a memory trace of a good experience to carry them through when they feel bored, frustrated and generally unsettled. Thus their behavior degenerates into impulsive drives—and what they want, they want immediately.

The culturally deprived persons have usually not developed either their reactive or their productive imaginations.[4] They cannot use their reactive imagination sufficiently well to benefit from past experiences.

If they are asked what happened a few minutes after it took place, they are apparently unable to look at it. Instead they blame something or someone else for the outcome. They are unable to, or do not, use their productive imagination to understand how their negative passivity and disruptive impulsive behavior provokes and annoys peers or authority figures. They are unlike the boy who explains, "I'm willing to admit that I fool around, that it isn't always the teacher's fault that I do, but I know when I'm going too far."

However, the explanation of their functioning on the basis of an underdeveloped ego is too simple. Instead their behavior is strange and paradoxical, since they display an ingenuity and vigilance in the use of their psychic energies. Many inner-city persons who are unable to cope with their impulses defend their impulse gratifications suddenly and with amazing efficiency. In their case instead of the ego using productive imagination in synthesizing desires, reality demands and social values, the ego supports impulsiveness.

Thus action of the ego in the culturally deprived works itself out in several ways. Impulse freedom is perceived so necessary that they become skilled in finding reasons for action against conscience. They use rationalization to maintain freedom for impulse expression. For example, "What else could I do? There was no way out." The ego acts in defense against change. If the teacher unwisely makes a direct attack on their rationalizations, they will withdraw, block and apparently become determined to make him do something to give them more justification for noncooperation and possibly hate.

Although these students are blind in the ways of the culturally conditioned, they are very much aware of the attitudes and feelings of the teacher but only in certain respects. Especially in their less intense moments they are unable to tell when the teacher is fair and reasonable and when he cares.

The teacher who proceeds with this group in the same manner as he would with the group whose members have the usual social learning is unlikely to succeed.

This does not mean that the teacher does not use group process with inner-city youth. Rather, it means that he uses it within a different framework. Instead of assuming, as he usually does, that (1) the students can control their impulses; (2) they can learn through experience because of strong memory traces and the use of their reactive imagination; (3) they can use their productive imagination to channel their desires constructively and to plan creatively, he recognizes that they have a minimal amount of these qualities.

Knowing this he establishes a framework which provides a good amount of security, sets limits on impulsive activity, and requires little use of imagination, but focuses on strengthening memory traces, self-control and teaching the relationship between freedom and responsibility.

He accomplishes these things in part by establishing boundaries of behavior and assuring the students a good experience if they live within these boundaries. At the same time he offers the opportunity to an individual or small group to have freedom to decide and do something on their own if they demonstrate that they can be responsible.

SUMMARY

He works with them always as a group. The individual is considered and treated as a member of the group. Group evaluation of behavior and learning is used as a means of progress. Recognition of self-control and group planning is given equal emphasis with other kinds of learning. The teacher proceeds to develop with them the skills and practices of group process.

More opportunity to plan activities and methods of procedures is given students as they show that they can use these experiences in a responsible way. The teacher takes opportunities as they arise to help them to be intelligent about what is taking place and to understand that they can have as much freedom, and only as much, as they are responsible for.

The teacher does not allow students to place him in the role of policing, punishing, or controlling. He works cooperatively as a special member of their group at all times. Gradually they come to see him as someone who can help them have a good experience, as a special one of them. This will take months to accomplish and there will be setbacks but the teacher believing in this method does not change in midstream for an inferior one.

When rightly used, group process in teaching has many advantages in helping students become whole persons.

In Changing Organizational Patterns

Before examining the function of group process in organizational change, it may be useful to place it in focus. To do this, such topics as the psychological and sociological attitudes of individuals toward change, the risks that are an integral part of change and nonchange, and the theories regarding how change takes place are used to clarify and illustrate conditions and problems inherent in organizational change.

THE SITUATION

Everyone knows that change is a fact of life. But often he knows this fact for someone else, not for himself. Stability, dependability and security encourage more comfortable thinking than flux, movement and unpredictability. Many of us are prone to accept the inequalities, inefficiencies and frustrations we know rather than move into an uncertain future. We are fearful of using our productive imaginations to envisage what might be.

This is true in organizations just as it is in persons, for organizations are composed of people. In organizations, and especially in church and school, we delegate our responsibilities to others—a board or a committee—and usually expect them to maintain things as they are. They have our blessing only as long as they introduce minor changes. Some of the board members want it this way and those who do not are soon under pressure to conform. Performing only with "the courage to be as a part," [5] persons of the former type begin to idealize the status quo and become almost fanatic in their defensiveness of the system. They tend to be suspicious of any member who proposes a major change in policy or methods.

On the other hand, any board or committee is likely to have members who are more concerned about their relationship with those who have power and influence than in what is best for the organization. Such members and persons change as their authorities change and they do so with minor difficulty. In this way they hope to retain their present benefits and to be in line for others in the future. Such persons are sometimes known as "party-line" changers.[6]

Because of reluctance to change on the part of many, there is frequently an inadequate examination by the membership of the situation. Conclusions are often based on opinion. A group may engage in action research and present representative and generally unbiased and authentic data but these data are not properly used. The members of the committee omit some of the data which do not conform to their formed conclusions, or they use other partial and biased data as influential in their decisions. They may also distort the meaning of the actual data presented.[7] Such behavior accounts in part for decisions by the committee different from those expected by the membership.

Change and the breadth of the time span of the members of the organization have a direct relationship. Some members have a broad time span with similar emphasis on past, present and future. They are more likely to observe conditions as they really are. They are in a better position to make reasonable judgments about present conditions and needed changes.

Some have narrowed their time span. They place greater emphasis on either the past or the present. In both instances they are inclined to be less interested and insightful about the future. Those who place their emphasis on the present accept change as it comes. They are unlikely to use available information in order to plan well for the future. Those who emphasize the past often do not recognize the changes which are taking place all around them. As far as possible they see the organization as being the same as it has always been. They use many forms of rationalization in order to avoid a consideration that change may be necessary. They may idealize the past, relinquishing or ruling out any idea that the present or future could possibly compare favorably with the "good old days." If they have spent many years in the organization the only kind of change which they entertain is a return to at least something similar to the part of the past which they have idealized.

Attitudes toward change in any organization are many-sided and complex. The more fearful or insecure the members, the more adverse the attitudes toward change will be. It is known that the most logical men can be quite illogical concerning an issue when the outcomes are perceived as threatening to their way of life.

CONFRONTING RISKS

Change presents risk. Risk can take many forms—a risk to our thought patterns, social patterns, financial patterns, patterns of belief, and patterns of behavior. These risks often appear more formidable to some persons than to others. For example, consider a church that may change the time of public worship on Sunday morning from 11 A.M. to 10 A.M. Some say, "Think of how early we would have to get up." Others say, "Why, church school would be at nine, the children would lose their rest, we couldn't have a leisurely Sunday morning breakfast, and we would never get the children there on time." Some stewards might say, "Our attendance will be sure to drop and our offerings would decrease."

The risks are generally perceived present only if a change is made. The risk taken by not making a change when it is the better part of wisdom to do so is often not considered seriously. Frequently, the assumption seems to be that there is no risk in continuing what has been done in the past. There is a failure to make the relationship between the societal and economic changes and their impact on things as they are. Many can discuss changes in beliefs in cultural mores and economic conditions and fail to relate these to the life of the organization of which they are a part.

On the other hand, many do not really confront risks. They do all that is possible to make themselves and their families secure. Then they remove themselves from the concerns of life, be these religious, social, economic or political. These persons are quite willing to leave important decisions to a board or committee. In so doing they may pride themselves on being liberal and democratic, or in having faith in their fellow man. This kind of behavior eventually forces them to resign themselves to accept whatever comes along. They may even be used by a power group with an ax to grind.

What is apparently not often realized is that the choice one makes is not between risk and no risk but, rather, between different kinds of risks. To live unmindful of this situation is to live in a small world with only the "courage to be as a part." It is a high price to pay for pseudo peace of mind.

However, it requires courage to accept the fact that life has built-in risk and that the making of decisions is the road to maturity and well-being. Perhaps the most difficult decision is one which accepts the fact that some things can be changed and some cannot. Perhaps some people too often conclude that something cannot be changed which actually could and should be changed by the use of perseverance and intelligent effort.

These many-sided aspects of the problem of risk-taking emphasize the necessity that a group working on change needs to be heterogeneous. Members of such a group can help one another to understand the various points of view and offer assistance in the development of positive attitudes toward change.

THEORIES OF CHANGE

A traumatic upset in an organization will induce several kinds of radical change, especially if such an upset is unexpected. The kinds of change and their results are generally unpredictable. They could lead to useful change or to disaster both for the organization and for the individuals who are a part of it.

The kind of change under consideration here is that which takes place gradually and may be planned or unplanned, constructive or destructive. With reference to this kind of change there are two streams of thought which are generally accepted. The first, and perhaps more common, is that change takes place in a stimulus-response relationship. An authority figure, a board of directors, or a situation decrees or encourages a change, offering some desirable reward for cooperation. If a situation induces a change which is advantageous to the organization or individual the result will encourage further change. In accordance with the reinforcement theory, a good result, a reward, or encouragement can be expected to motivate the organization or individual to continue with the same procedures toward the same goal.

It is assumed that change is only an intellectual process. It is thus considered to be involved chiefly with the cognitive processes. This method of inducing change in an organization, i.e., from the top down, often comes under criticism as highly impersonal and manipulative.[8] It is the usual theoretical stance and method of what Gibb has called "defensive management."[9] Organizations which use such authoritarian methods in which change is imposed have no interest in organic group process. Many still deliberately "use the attractive symbols of democracy, participation, man-to-man discussion, group discussion, etc., to create the desired atmosphere within which they can smoothly manipulate the attiudes of their employees, retain their loyalty and still run the business 'as it should be run' without irritating influences from below."[10]

Much of the change which results from such authoritarian methods based on association theory of learning (change associated with rewards) and extrinsic motivation (coming from outside the person) is not genuine change. It has the appearance of genuineness but often the individual, board, committee, supervisors or organization may be changing for reasons of expediency. The change is phenotypical or superficial.

The second stream of thought places importance on the total involvement and free choice of the individual. It assumes that genuine change does not take place unless the new set of values is freely chosen by the individual or group. Genuine change takes place when the individual is free to do otherwise. In contrast to the first, which places primary emphasis on the cognitive, this approach places emphasis on the integration of the emotional (values and valences), cognitive (thinking, perception and memory) and motoric, with special emphasis on the emotional.

Lewin and Grabbe discuss the second position in this manner: "The re-educative (change) process affects the individual in three ways. It changes his cognitive structure, the way he sees the physical and social worlds, including all his facts, concepts, beliefs and expectations. It modifies his valences and values and these embrace both his attractions and aversions to groups and group standards, his feelings in regard to status differences, and his reactions to sources of approval or disapproval. And it affects motoric action, involving the degree of the individual's control over his physical and social movements." [11]

Motivation to change stems from within. Thus this theory of self-change (intrinsic motivation) relies upon the perception of the individual (or those responsible for the well-being of the organization) of the incongruity between the actual and the desirable. The assumption is that progress will be made toward the goal which the individual or those in the organization choose and that there is in all cases the capability of examining and evaluating the related alternatives.

Organizations which change and progress through the resetting and attainment of goals coming from within make wide use of organic group process. Their ideas of change have their roots in the concepts of field theory (needs arising in the field [environment] and worked on by all concerned), intrinsic motivation, total involvement and genuine self-change. As previously indicated, Gibb used the term "defensive management" to describe the aggregate or authoritarian group; he uses the term "participative management" to describe the organic or true group. He uses this term to describe the method of using many small groups cutting across staff and line positions in industry, and across lay and professional positions in church and social service organizations.

STRATEGIES FOR CHANGE

Each of the two theories discussed above has its particular strategy for change. The more common strategy is based upon the association theory of learning, authoritarian relationships and aggregate groups. The method is basically the same whether the organization is a home, church, social service, business or industrial organization. Of course the titles of the individuals, boards or committees differ but the methods which they use are similar.

For instance in the church setting, the minister may decide that to increase giving, the church should initiate an every-member canvass. He discusses (sells) the idea with the chairman of the Official Board. The chairman talks over (sells) the idea with the heads of committees on the board. At the next meeting of the Official Board it becomes the chief item on the agenda. It is introduced by the chairman and supported by the heads of committees. There is an aggregate group discussion in which questions are asked and opinions offered. No serious opposition is expected and no alternative seriously considered as a possibility. The matter is agreed upon and the chairman may suggest that each board member call his ten key members to discuss (sell) the idea before the congregational meeting.

If the board likes to think of itself as being liberal and democratic, it will be suggested to each of the ten key members that they get together a small group to discuss (sell) the idea before the congregational meeting. These small groups of seven to ten people will meet, perhaps in the key member's home. The aggregate group will hear the idea, its rationale, advantages, stage of planning. Questions will be asked, the idea may be challenged by one or two, but since it is considered a good idea by the Official Board and other members it will be generally accepted although less enthusiastically by some. Refreshments will be served, the conversation will turn to golf, stocks, travel and the latest recipes and the members will then depart.

At the congregational meeting which may be held in the sanctuary, the chairman of the Official Board will supply a well-prepared rationale for the change, emphasize all the committees and groups who favor it, and express regrets that all could not attend the small-group meetings.

Opportunity will be given for discussion (questions and answers). Questions of information will be asked and responded to. One or two may challenge the idea but they will not be responded to, or a "way around" the objection will be presented by a member of the congregation (perhaps a committee head, who would like to be the next Official Board chairman). A vote will be called for "ayes" and "nays," and the chairman will announce in a matter-of-fact tone, "Carried," and will thank each member for coming and for his cooperation. The meeting will be adjourned.

There will of course be minor variations from congregation to congregation and from situation to situation. The idea of change may originate in the Official Board or in a similar body. In this case the first step is to obtain strong backing from the other board members for the idea by phone call, at the golf club, or over coffee. Then the idea is introduced at the regular meeting of the board for the purpose of discussing (selling) it with the minister. He may ask questions, supply information, express a doubt or two, but he is unlikely to oppose outright the change, especially when he discovers it is favored by most of the board members.

This method of change is rarely examined. When it is,

it is deemed to be democratic, efficient and necessary. There is little recognition that it is manipulative, that the change has been imposed and accepted only cognitively and frequently unintelligently. If the change imposed requires sacrifice of time and money, such as a new education building, a new organ, or a redecoration of the church interior, there is often a strong reaction. It is a common understanding among clergy that if such a major change is carried out, the minister's own position will be in jeopardy. Nevertheless this is the most common method of bringing about change both within the church and without.

There is another method of change, only infrequently used, and considered by many to be inefficient, slow and time-consuming. However, when it is used, the change is acceptable, intelligent and progressive. The participants are fully involved, highly cooperative and enthusiastic.

This method is based upon field theory and the need-experience method of learning. It is democratic and communication is through the use of the organic group process. The idea which may result in change could originate with any member of the church. In a church in which the offerings are not sufficient for the church to meet its expenses and progress, a member may decide he wishes to understand the situation fully. He brings his concern to the attention of a trained group leader and solicits his help in forming and leading a group to discuss the causes of the financial situation of the church. An announcement is made and a small group of five to seven members is formed with plans to meet weekly over several months. The members of this group may explore what the church means to them and become acquainted with the financial situation. During this time they also come to know one another better and they establish some sense of groupness. Their purposes for meeting become clear to each one and they learn to listen and to try to understand one another's ideas.

They are now ready to relate to others and to carry their discussion further. They invite into the group a member who is well acquainted with the financial situation—perhaps the church treasurer or the financial secretary. They may also invite a member of the Official Board. When they do this, they may face a problem. Those they invite are not accustomed to the exploration and discussion of a problem without taking a vote and coming to a decision. Their expectation is that they are invited in order to be sold something. So uneasy are they, that one of them may ask "What is it you are trying to sell?" They are bewildered and skeptical when told that no one is trying to sell anything to anyone.

The original group continues to meet and invites other church leaders to participate with them. In this manner a large number become informed concerning the church and its finances. However, the knowledge of, and interest developed in, the support of the church is actually secondary to the sense of belonging, feeling of adequacy and openness to one another which results from this kind of group process.

As an outcome, the group may ask the Official Board to entertain a discussion of some changes which they and others who discussed it consider helpful. If the board concludes that the idea for change has value, the original group will plan to provide opportunity for every member to participate in its consideration. They will be invited to join in small groups of seven, meeting at least three separate times not more than a week apart. The members of the original group will act as leaders of these small groups along with others whose interest and ability enable them to lead small groups for this purpose. If these small groups reach a consensus in favor of the change, a congregational vote may be taken in a manner in accord with church policy.

Of course churches and other organizations vary in the way they use organic group process. The general principles and methods are similar. A problem or need is recognized by an individual or group. With the help of a trained leader, clarification, analysis, more information and more discussion emerge. The original group is expanded and others experience the sense of belonging and feeling of purposefulness. Gradually many have this group experience and become informed.

If these groups conclude that the changes discussed are necessary, steps are taken which ensure that all members have an opportunity to become informed through this process. This is then followed by congregational action if it is still deemed wise.

If change is a result in this method of using the democratic process and organic groups, it is a by-product. It follows experience in a small group in which the members have become mature in self-understanding and understanding of others and also in the securing and evaluation of information. It is assumed that genuine change involves the whole person; it cannot be imposed, and it becomes an actuality through a growth process which is best furthered in small-group experiences.

In various organizations where the nature and possibilities of organic group process are understood its use is growing. It has been found to be one of the best means for increasing understanding and harmony both within and between departments, committees, boards and job areas. The kind of interpersonal communication thus fostered is excellent preparation for the invitation and handling of change with minimal apprehensiveness and resistance.

PREPARATION FOR CHANGE

Since it is now recognized that rapid change is a fact of life, an ongoing readiness and means of change become a necessity. There is widespread acceptance of the use of democratic procedures for the initiation of change. But there is only minimal understanding of the concept of change and of the democratic method. Some of the lack of understanding is centered on the meaning of change. Frequently it is considered a simple variable and all change thus assumed to be equally valuable. The democratic method is assumed to be only a method requiring certain skills but no change in perception and attitudes; thus an authoritarian person believes he may use the democratic method through the acquisition of some know-how.

Such lack of understanding demonstrates itself in our educational methods in church, school, industry and home. The illustration provided of the change to the method of "every-member canvass" for the raising of church funds demonstrates it. The Official Board in this instance considered the method used to be democratic. They based their conclusion on the fact that every member had a chance to know, that they used small groups, and voted on it at a congregational meeting.

Regardless of the organization such assumptions and practices reduce persons to objects. They breed fear, apprehension, resistance in some; in others resignation, aimlessness and loss of meaning; and in still others hostility, aggression and refined means of sabotage.

It is time that organic small groups become an integral part of the functioning of all organizations. Organizations[12] moving in this direction have found their efforts worthwhile both in the personal well-being of their members or employees and in the quantity and quality of their productivity. Much more knowledge is needed, but some of this must be gained through experience.

To move from pseudo-democracy with its camouflaged aggregate group life to real democracy with its true organic group life still remains a difficult re-educative effort. This transformation is a slow process because it depends on the knowledge and readiness of persons to change. Each organization will move at its own rate. Although operational conditions vary among organizations, the following minimal requirements indicate the nature of a working reality.

1. Leaders must be trained in group process. To ensure a sufficient number of leaders, each organization should have an ongoing program for the training of leaders.

2. There must be a sufficient number of small groups of from seven to fifteen persons to provide an opportunity for each person in the organization, school, church, industry or business to be a member of a group.

3. There must be heterogeneous groups cutting across all levels of work and types of responsibility.

4. Groups should meet regularly—weekly, or at least semimonthly, and over a sufficient length of time to become mature functioning groups.

5. Discussions should be open-ended, with the majority of subjects chosen by the members of the group itself. These will naturally include a discussion of changes desired by the group members.

6. The leader should assist the members to understand the process, improve their functioning, solve problems and engage in distributive leadership.

7. There should be provision of opportunity and encouragement for members to become trained as leaders

with the intention of serving in organizational groups in this capacity.

The use of organic group process recognizes that the employees, members, students, faculty, supervisors, etc., are persons first, and second working in an organization.

With Focus on the Church

How do the lay member and the professional church leader decide what to do about the groups in the church? What kinds of decisions should each make before he can be reasonably sure that he is doing what is most useful? Each will ask different questions in terms of the purpose he has in mind. Neither should become involved in groups casually, haphazardly or unintelligently. Each should consider groups in terms of his own needs, the service he may be able to give and the purposes of the church.

Each will address himself to one or more of the following considerations. (1) Why use organic groups? (2) For what purposes should group process be used? (3) How do I prepare to lead groups? (4) How do I improve my leadership of groups? (5) How do I decide which kind of group to use? (6) How do I decide to use a particular leader? (7) How do I plan for a sustaining leadership of small groups?

WHY USE ORGANIC GROUPS?

Aggregate groups differ from organic groups in the following significant ways. In an aggregate group, the interaction is generally two-way from the leader to the member and from the member to the leader. An organic group has a three-way process from member to member, members to leader, and leader to members.

The leader of an aggregate group often uses a prepared agenda and has planned specific outcomes instead of developing the agenda and planning the outcomes cooperatively with the members. Decisions are reached by a majority rule instead of by consensus. The ideal members are those who generally conform to the ideas and plans of the leader. Occasionally a member of the aggregate group may suggest some minor changes, but the organic group thrives on the expression of creative differences and there is a readiness to change if and when change seems appropriate.

Organic groups differ from aggregate groups in their interpersonal relations, the feeling tone, and the psychological climate. In an organic group, there is a sensitive, cooperative relationship. The feeling that one must perform in order to be accepted gradually gives place to the realization that one is accepted on the basis of his personhood. In the organic group, one has the experience of being listened to, of being able to say what he truly feels and thinks. There is an atmosphere of trust. There is also a growing sense of loving concern for each member in the group accompanied by a sense of responsibility for helping each other and the progress of the group as a whole.

The church has always been a natural setting for groups. The majority of the activities in the church are carried out by groups. Most of these, however, are aggregate groups and are not organic in nature. Boards, committees, church school classes, work groups and agenda-planning groups seldom become organic groups. They become efficient planning groups; they get things done; but they lack the developed and developing qualities of acceptance, trust, loving concern and responsibility. In their midst is secular, low-keyed competition rather than the ingredients that characterize communication in love.

When religious leaders turn skeptical about groups or conclude they have too many groups already, they are confusing the aggregate secularized group with the true organic group and its possibilities for grasping the transcendent in life which goes beyond what can be heard, felt and seen.

FOR WHAT PURPOSES SHOULD GROUP PROCESS BE USED?

Group process in some form is the essence of communication. In secular society the process of aggregate groups may be efficient in terms of secular goals while at the same time depersonalizing those who are involved. In the religious society the same aggregate group process may slowly destroy the interpersonal relationships by which the message of the church becomes fact.

Organic group process is basic to every aspect of church life. It should be the basis and method of the educational, social and spiritual life of the church. Churches large and small do well when they find ways to organize their memberships in small groups. These groups should be formed with great care. They should be heterogeneous in their composition with reference to age, educational and vocational backgrounds. There is a transition from the present aggregate or authoritarian and pseudo-democratic forms of organization in many churches to a truly organic and democratic organization. This transition needs to be made slowly and in keeping with the readiness of the individual congregations.

HOW TO PREPARE TO LEAD

As a member of your church, you are interested in becoming a group leader. You would like to use this method with some group in the church. You are a college graduate and although you have been in many groups, you have never participated in a truly organic or democratic group. How do you begin?

Examine the groups in which you are now participating.

What process is being used to reach decisions? What is being done to help the members relate to one another? What do you think are the aims of the leader? What does he do to try to realize these aims? What do you do in the group? How do you feel about it? What would you like to do and how would you like to feel?

Read widely about groups. Try to discern the various purposes of groups; how groups differ in relation to their purposes; what methods are used to secure involvement of the members; how the leader functions in various groups.

Try to understand yourself in relation to groups. How do you behave as a group member? How do you think you would like to function as a leader? Would you like to ask questions, make suggestions, evaluate occasionally, or make interpretations of how well the group is doing or what it should be doing? Do you get a great deal of satisfaction from having others look to you for information, suggestions or plans?

On the other hand, would you rather be a leader who does almost none of these things, but tries to assist the members by clarifying statements, reflecting the meaning of others' comments, linking together ideas with similar meanings, summarizing when you think it is necessary? Would you be satisfied to be a leader who rarely asks a question and gives brief information only when it seems very necessary? Do you receive satisfaction from seeing a member begin to participate who formerly seemed inhibited and withdrawn, or from seeing a group reach a good decision and make plans for carrying it out with very little help from you?

These are important considerations, since they help you to recognize your source of satisfaction as a group leader. Knowing this, you are better able to decide the kind of leadership training you should seek. You may now wish to examine more critically the different types of leadership functioning in the various groups. Determine the kind of leadership which would be required in order that you may do the things you would most enjoy. This kind of leadership functioning has the best chance of satisfying your needs. Also determine the kind of leadership you feel would be most helpful to the members. If this is not the same kind of leadership that you decided you would most enjoy, are you willing and able to change?

The next step is to secure training. Care must be exercised in doing this. You must carefully weigh the similarities and differences between a group-centered group and a sensitivity or T group. When you have decided which group would be most useful to you, secure any possible information of the group experience. You may wish to do this in several ways. You may talk to a member who has participated in the kind of group in which you are considering enrollment. You may talk with the leader asking him how he functions and what takes place in the group. Discuss the matter with the director of education and/or pastor of the church.

Membership in a group needs to be supplemented by supervised practice in leading groups. It is advisable to have the responsibility of leading groups of different sizes, and groups with different purposes. Your training with a professional leader should extend over a minimum of two ten-week periods and should then be followed by a supervised internship in which you have the responsibility of leading a group.

HOW TO IMPROVE YOUR LEADERSHIP

You are the lay leader of an activity in the church. You would like to be able to use the democratic method in your work with church groups. You have studied group process in related courses extending over four quarters of university work, part of which was an internship experience.

You recognize that your leadership is authoritarian and only occasionally and to a small degree democratic. You plan what is to be discussed, and what the outcomes of the discussions should be. You are firm, kind and efficient. You ask for members' ideas regarding what to do and how to do it. After hearing these, you decide what to do and call for a vote when you are uncertain. You haven't thought much about the process. You are interested only in getting things done. You haven't tried much to improve the way you do things. You like the idea of organic groups. How do you begin?

Proceed slowly. Be patient, recognizing that you will need to learn some skills and that it will take time and effort if you are to become a democratic person. Try to become aware of how you are presently operating in the group. At the same time, try to recognize those kinds of plans, issues or problems concerning which you have some feeling of confidence. With these, you may be able to accept more than one way of working them out.

After this preliminary period of getting acquainted with yourself, you might proceed in the following manner. As the need arises for interaction with others concerning any phase of the program, ask yourself if this is something you could truly ask the group to discuss. That is, do you feel sufficiently secure about this that you could entertain many points of view and accept a result different from or in addition to any that you had conceived? If the need arose, could you share your status authority to the point of allowing others to be responsible for certain aspects of the activity?

Implicit in this venture is the assumption that when a matter is presented for discussion, it is no longer phony. Instead, each member has the privilege and the responsibility which go with significantly deciding the future of this group.

Also implicit is the assumption that a matter will not be presented for discussion if the leader has already decided what the outcome should be. As a leader, you will use your productive imagination to decide whether the matter at hand is one which you must decide or one which can be dealt with cooperatively by the group.

Some matters may not be appropriate for discussion for one or more of the following reasons. (1) The matter may be one which is "fixed" by institutional policy. That is, you and your group may not have the freedom to make any changes. (2) The subject to be discussed may be something concerning which you conclude you are not psychologically able to permit a cooperative decision. (3) You may conclude that the group for one or several reasons is unable to enter into the decision-making process (e.g., immaturity, lack of experience, inability to assume the responsibility that accompanies making the decision). As a leader, you should not make this an excuse for not engaging in cooperative decision-making.

As time progresses, you will be improving your skills in communication. That is, you will experiment with using clarification, reflection and occasionally summarization. You will rely less on direct questioning. You will avoid the evaluation of responses and interpretation of ideas or feelings. The members will become more and more interested in the process and perceive you as a flexible person and a special member of the group.

You will also have directed their interest and attention to the process and its improvement. You will have an observer who will report on each session for the purpose of making members aware of what is taking place and planning ways for improving. You and the remaining members will participate for this purpose also.

After some weeks, you will observe an increasing acceptance of one another. There will also be indications of interest in helping one another, a growing sense of responsibility for others, and a concern for the well-being of the group. The members enjoy themselves together and you will notice that their acceptance and feeling of togetherness are also transferred to activities outside those of the group.

You can encourage this attitude of acceptance, trust and sense of responsibility through your own openness and sharing.

DECIDING ON THE KIND OF GROUP PROCESS TO USE

You are a director of religious education in the church. You would like to have a professional lead some groups. How may you decide to invite a group-centered or a sensitivity-group leader? You would like the members of the group to lead small educational groups upon completion of the training. You would like them to be sensitive, understanding leaders.

Unless you have recently studied the method and process of each of these groups, you may wish to begin by becoming familiar with the literature on each kind of group. You will find it helpful to address yourself to such questions as the following: Which kind of group will provide the most experience to prospective leaders of groups? Which will help members become intelligent about the various skills of group process and assist them in the use of these skills? Which group uses the process that you perceive to be most useful in the church setting?

You are encouraging certain church members to participate in the training experience. What are they like? Has each a good self-concept? Does each examine his motivations and behavior in relation to acceptable standards of behavior related to the principles of the teaching of the church? Can I and should I discuss with each his perception of the experiences in the various groups with regard to what he thinks might be more helpful to him?

You will have to relate the cooperative decision of your member prospects and yourself to the professional leadership available. You may have to search diligently in order to obtain a professional leader for the kind of experience you desire. You will not be wise to substitute the leader of a very different orientation just because he is available and/or aggressive concerning his point of view.

You may wish to examine these guidelines and then come to conclusions concerning those which will become your own. Your prospects for training may be somewhat inflexible and to some degree withdrawn; perhaps they make decisions only on the basis of what is expedient and useful and may rarely look at their values and interpersonal relationships. In this case, a T group or sensitivity training might be considered, especially if your contacts with them would indicate that the prospective group members have ego strength. The assumption underlying the above is that these persons may not be moved to try to understand themselves and others unless they are pressured to do so. The safety and acceptance of the group-centered group may not be sufficient motivation.

However, those who do choose a sensitivity group or a T group should not be expected to become more intelligent about necessary skills or increase to an appreciable degree their ability to perform as leaders of groups from this encounter. These persons would need further experiences in which they gradually gain skills in leading groups. Those persons who experience T-group or sensitivity training will naturally desire to conduct groups using the same method. Thus you will need to decide if you wish to have sensitivity groups or T groups as the training method of leadership and action in your church groups. You should ask yourself whether or not this method is one which could be transferred helpfully to the church setting. Of course, all of those who enter this training experience may not become leaders. The problem, then, is that they are generally unhappy in other groups if the leaders do not proceed in T-group or sensitivity-group fashion.

The difficulty experienced by those who are expected to become group-centered leaders after a T-group experience is chiefly one of becoming group-centered persons. They are probably as authoritarian in their attitudes and behavior following T-group training as they were before entering it.

The other choices you may have are the authoritarian, participation training (the Indiana Plan), democratic group or group-centered group.

The authoritarian pattern is probably the one now used in groups throughout most of the church activities. You may wish to continue with it, hoping to improve it, but before making a firm decision you may wish to analyze what is now taking place. In doing this, it could be helpful to set up certain questions as a basis for the analysis. Some of the questions might be the following: (1) Is the decision-making efficient? (2) Are members responsible in carrying out these decisions? (3) Are the decisions of a quality which could be considered representative of an organic group? Another set of questions would relate themselves to the quality of the interpersonal relations among the members. What is happening to the psychological development of the members? Are the individual members gaining in self-understanding and in their understanding of other members? Are the members improving in their listening to each other? Are the members developing a sense of caring and responsibility for one another? Are the members developing a sense of adequacy in their relation with others?

Participation training (the Indiana Plan) is designed to improve the leadership and membership skills in discussion. It does not claim to improve members' self-understanding and their understanding of others, nor does it try to achieve this. No attempt is made to develop groupness, a sense of belonging, caring or responsibility. Some of these qualities develop indirectly and incidentally. You may wish to consider this form of training if you are only interested in your groups becoming more efficient discussion groups.

Your choice may be between democratic and group-centered groups. The leader in each of these groups must desire to become a democratic or group-centered person. This requires a kind of personality change which takes place only gradually, since the developmental experiences of your potential leaders will have been in authoritarian environments for the most part. If you are chiefly interested in developing leaders who believe in cooperative planning and are capable of using it in helping members gain a sense of adequacy and some feeling of responsibility, you may choose the democratic pattern of leadership training.

You will consider group-centered leadership training if you are interested in leaders of church activities who will give freedom of choice to members in proportion to their responsibility. This method provides much opportunity for the member to gain some feeling of worth and self-understanding and to develop a sense of caring and responsibility for others.

You may wish to consider the use of groups not only for

educational purposes but also for counseling. You may see the use of groups as a means of extending individual counseling and also as a kind of experience which may be more useful to some than individual or one-to-one counseling. Group counseling has inherent potentialities for therapeutic change which are not present in individual counseling. Among these are: (1) a community in which the person may test his evolving attitudes and ideas; (2) the motivation which results from the acceptance of peers and the experience of his changing attitudes; (3) the skills of communication with others which improve his possibilities of developing genuine interpersonal relationships; (4) the encouragement which follows from the participation with others in trying to resolve one another's conflicts; and (5) the acceptance and understanding of peers with the resulting sense of safety and belonging which support the process of introspection and expression of feeling in depth.

You will, of course, engage in the same study and consideration and exercise the same caution as in your decisions regarding the use and choice of leadership regarding educational groups. In this case, however, you are not asking if this group experience will provide practice in leadership and membership skills and in the understanding of group process itself. Instead, you will ask if this group can facilitate the members' understanding of their problems, supply the incentive to do something about them and offer experiences in reality-testing their evolving changes in attitudes and behaviors. You are concerned with what kind of group will induce the necessary involvement and provide the most useful psychological environment for the member to examine himself and set new goals.

You will not assume that all members will benefit from the same kind of group. Some may benefit more from a T group or sensitivity group and some from a group-centered group. At this stage of development and understanding there is no researched method of determining which persons will derive more benefit from one than another. Examination of the theory and methods of each leads to the following extrapolated and logical conclusions. The person who has developed his depth potential may not need to be pressured into confrontation with himself. He needs instead a psychological climate in which competition and acceptance in relation to performance are removed. In a climate of unconditional acceptance and safety he confronts himself in an effort to understand himself, his relation to others and their relation to him. Such a person stands to gain more from a group-centered group. This is the kind of person who, in making important decisions, asks not only the questions of expediency, utility and practicality, but also the questions of justice, fairness, mercy, rightness and personal responsibility.

Persons who rarely ask the questions of depth but whose decision-making is dependent upon expediency, utility, and practicality could be expected to need a T group or sensitivity group to force them to explore their lives and living in depth.

It should be recognized that the risks of psychological damage are present in the "pressure cooker" experience of the T group and sensitivity group, but virtually absent in the group-centered group.

It should be obvious, then, that you will discuss the matter of choice of group carefully with each of those who anticipate joining a group.

DECIDING ON A PARTICULAR LEADER

Assuming that you have decided upon the kind of group leader you would like to have work with groups in the church, you will need criteria as a basis for helping you to decide whether or not a particular leader is a good choice. You will want to know his training, the method he uses and his experience. Despite the favorable reports you may hear concerning the work of lay people in this field, you will hesitate to engage one of them. Rather, you will attempt to secure information about the leader, and if he is well qualified, he will provide it. You will try to secure a college-trained person who is a graduate of a program in counseling psychology or in counseling and guidance. Also, he should have had several courses in the theory and practice of the group method which he plans to use. He should have experience in leading groups over a period of several years.

You will discuss with him whether or not he specializes in educational groups, in group counseling, or in group therapy. If you are interested in securing help for persons with psychological problems you will look for a leader whose experience has been in group counseling or group therapy. If you are interested in securing a leader who will train members to become in turn leaders of educational groups, you will select one whose chief experience has been in educational groups.

Since sensitivity and T-group trainers vary widely in the methods they use, it would be well to discuss the method to be used thoroughly before making a decision. Persons who have had a course with the leader can often offer useful information also. Discuss their experience, asking questions which will help you to understand what took place. It is also important to secure some idea of what carryover the experience has had in their daily living in terms of feelings, attitudes and activities.

PLANNING FOR A SUSTAINING LEADERSHIP

Church leaders who use small groups to improve the quality of the interpersonal relations of members and to increase the relevance and vitality of church groups will recognize the need of ongoing plans for training those who can serve as leaders of small groups. The ideal they envision is having a leader available as the need arises and thus being in a position to use the small-group method for short-term and long-term needs. They recognize many occasions when a small-group experience could greatly facilitate problem-solving and the development of attitudinal understanding.

To make this possible, you must have a continuous and ongoing opportunity for members to train as leaders. There are several ways in which you may develop such a program. You will begin by securing the services of the professional leader chosen in the manner previously discussed. You will invite church members—some of whom may be leaders—to participate in the training experience with the understanding that they will eventually lead or co-lead other groups in the church. From seven to twelve persons would make a suitably sized group. Ideally the group would meet twice a week for two hours over a ten-week period. Two such training periods would be minimal preparation for any member. Each member would then become responsible under professional supervision to lead a small group. This supervised experience should be of at least ten weeks' duration. Not all beginning leaders require the same amount of help. It is possible for the professional leader to supervise more than one beginning leader if the groups meet in adjacent rooms.

After one year of continuous experience a trained leader may undertake the training of a small group with occasional help from a professional.

9 *STUDYING THE GROUP*

Research in the Local Setting

Experience and common sense are useful and necessary in the study of the group, but unless more than these can be brought to bear directly on troublesome problems, questions will be formulated and conclusions drawn which are inadequate. Research can supply more dependable and accurate information. It is a means of reducing the probability of harmful assumptions and procedures which limit the possibilities of constructive accomplishments.

The group leader should, with the help of the members, engage himself in three ongoing types of study. (1) He should study published research to become informed of the trends. He and any of his group members who are qualified should examine various research designs as a means of stimulating productive imagination in regard to possible and helpful studies in their own groups. (2) He should plan informal research cooperatively to function in the several areas of group process. At the same time, he must maintain a reasonable expectancy. He knows that research has its limitations and that subtle variables cannot all be accounted for. He is aware that these will continue to challenge any form of empirical measurement.

CONSIDERATIONS

In deciding the extent and nature of the research he contemplates, the leader should examine possible kinds of research in relation to the information about groups and group process which would be useful to him and the group members. He should ask how important formal research may be. Will it provide needed guidelines or information? Does he have the training or could he secure the needed help to carry it out? Do the conditions under which he conducts groups lend themselves comfortably to this kind of activity? Could he avoid some of the prevalent weaknesses of much of group-counseling research? To what specific degree could the following conditions be met: proper control groups, long-term criterion measures, a series of group meetings to justify an expectation of change, and experienced group leaders to help improve the research and increase the numbers involved.

If there are reasons to assume that these conditions could be adequately met he may decide to engage in some formal research. If not, he should concentrate on doing informal studies of the group which could be highly useful.

If after such preliminary considerations he decides to do some formal research, he should go further in his thinking and planning. He should examine his hunches carefully to determine which could be expected to obtain useful results and so would be worth the necessary time and effort. He would then review several research designs to determine which is the best "fit" for what he wants to do. He evaluates the design to determine if it is congruent with the assumptions and method he uses.

He tests his thinking further by subjecting his plan to these queries: Is the problem of sufficient importance that the outcomes could have significant results? Are the necessary conditions for conducting the research those which are ongoing and integral to the present group functioning? Is it reasonable to expect that the degree of member involvement will assure the validity of the outcomes? Will feedback be relevant? Can feedback be provided in a manner directly useful to the groups? To what degree can one account for the important variables in order to have general acceptance for the validity of the outcomes? To what degree is it reasonable to anticipate that the outcomes could be used in future group functioning?

In choosing a problem for research the leader may wish to confer with other group leaders, teachers, administrators, group members and perhaps others with whom he is associated in the organization.

He should recognize that formal research will require considerable time and energy and therefore he should not be tempted to engage in this activity if it forces him to limit himself in the actual time he gives to working with groups.

PROBLEMS

There are further problems and considerations concerned with the research itself. They revolve around such issues as the kind of studies and their purpose, professional assistance, validity and application of the results.

Many of the studies are enumerative and descriptive. Such studies lend themselves to easy observation and measurement but progress should go beyond these. Research should also be done for the purpose of understanding the conditions of behavioral change, the means of gaining insight into one's problems and making realistic decisions. Such kinds of analytic research are vague, intangible and difficult. It is hoped that they would be viewed as a challenge. The development of such techniques as the self and self-ideal Q sort[1] brings this more within the realm of possibility. These techniques ask the respondee to react not to a questionnaire, but instead from within his own frame of reference regarding what he decides is significant.

Another problem is the defining of the purpose of

group process in such a manner as to lend itself to research. The criterion against which to evaluate the efficiency of group process is a major problem. When the group leader is able to disentangle himself from the easier, less useful enumerative and descriptive research, he focuses upon meanings and cause-and-effect relationships. He then has the difficult problem of first explaining and then defining accurately what it is he plans to measure. His definition must finally be stated in a testable hypothesis. An illustration of this is Carl Rogers' definition of therapeutic personality change.[2]

Some group leaders will desire and need professional assistance. The leader would be wise to exercise caution in this matter. Not infrequently, a professional outside the group and the organization is invited to plan, conduct and evaluate the research. Such a person may have his own purposes which do not include the objective of the group leader, or perhaps even that of the organization. The group members remain largely uninformed concerning the research. They participate because they are expected to do so and may remain apathetic or resentful toward the whole undertaking.

There is a strong tendency toward apathy and resentment when the methodology of the research desired is beyond the competence of the group leader or others interested in the organization. They are capable of planning the goals, formulating hypotheses and setting up criteria but incapable of initiating, executing and evaluating. In such instances it is wise to ask the help of specialists in research methodology. Such specialists should be invited to assist only in a cooperative capacity. This means that they advise concerning the investigation itself, supervise the statistical analysis, and assist in the interpretation of the results[3] to the initiators and planners of the research.

Problems in validity focus on the sample, the involvement of the subjects and their anonymity. Not only should the sample have a good degree of randomness but also care should be taken to make sure that the subjects in the sample are representative of those for whom the leader plans to use the results. Heterogeneous groups may provide a better sample upon which to draw conclusions concerning those outside the sample group.

Without the interested involvement of the subjects there can be little validity in the results. The research may be worse than a waste of effort unless the subjects feel personally involved and interested in knowing the results in relation to their self-becoming and the group development. The subjects or members involved when they share in planning the research objectives, voluntarily participate, remain anonymous, and receive feedback in a form which they can use.

In a study of the group in the local situation the member's anonymity is of major importance. Regardless of the high degree of group cohesiveness it frees the members to be unhesitatingly open and honest, a necessity for valid results. Planning with the group to establish and maintain anonymity can be an important learning experience.

Care must be taken in applying the results of research to one's group. The group leader must satisfy himself regarding at least the following points: Was the research which was done based on the same theory and method as he himself uses? Was the experience of group process common to the subjects and the members in his groups? Was the sample of subjects in the study sufficiently random to be similar in this regard to his groups? What means were taken to assure the involvement of the participants? Did the participants remain anonymous? Was the experiment conducted over a period sufficiently long for change to be a reasonable outcome? Did the group leaders who conducted the groups have training and experience similar to his own?

The greater the number of positive answers to these queries, the greater will be the leader's assurance that the results of the research could be applied to his own groups. The leader who conducts research using his own groups does not need to be concerned with some of these queries. On the other hand, he has different concerns which are just as important. These concerns revolve around the problems of a leader being a participant in his own research. He cannot be as objective as the situation demands. It is questionable to what degree his participation influences the results. All he can do is take precautions to make sure that he does not knowingly engage in any activity which might lead to a distortion of the results.

Methods of Studying the Group

ACTION RESEARCH

Over the past two decades new methods for the study of groups have evolved from the refinement of observational techniques. Among these methods are those used in the study of the current ongoing relationships within the group. The most useful among them may generally be described as various forms of action research. Each method is slightly different but all have the same basic assumption.

Action research differs from formal or fundamental research in significant ways. Some of the major emphases of this research are the following: (1) It begins from an urgent need and with the intention of applying results toward the improvement of practice in the actual setting. (2) It is planned by the members and the leader with or without the aid of research specialists. (3) There is a developmental design with the hypothesis and method subject to modification during the course of the action program. (4) Its usefulness is in terms of the extent to which methods and findings make possible improvement in practice in a particular situation.[4]

CRITICAL-INCIDENT TECHNIQUE

One of these methods which makes improvement in practice possible is the critical-incident technique. A critical incident is a sample of the interaction, the result of which greatly influences the growth of the group. Good [5] describes these incidents as the use of direct observations which have special significance in solving practical problems and developing broad psychological principles. To be most useful the development of criteria is necessary as a guide in the selection of incidents for study.

Better results follow if the method is carried out in a systematic manner. Flanagan[6] lists the following five steps in the critical-incident procedures: (1) determining the general aim of the activity in the form of a brief statement; (2) developing plans and specifications for collecting factual incidents; (3) collecting data and reporting the incident in an interview or as written by the observer; (4) analyzing data in an effective and practical summary; and (5) interpreting and reporting a statement of the requirements of the activity.

This method is considered to have some unique values which are superior to other methods: (1) it places categories of human behavior on an empirical basis; (2) it provides a realistic base for a variety of evaluation techniques, although the incidents do not constitute a measurement instrument of themselves; and (3) incidents serve as a source of the raw material out of which evaluation items are constructed.[7]

During the fifth meeting the group discussed the topic of involvement. The members explored its nature, the kinds of involvement, and the reasons why some persons involve themselves more than others. They concluded that involvement was so important that they should develop some method of studying it.

They planned to record several sessions on tape and to analyze the critical incidents. They recognized the need of criteria as a basis for analysis and for the purpose of comparing one incident with another. Several members had heard of the critical-incident method and they volunteered to bring back information to the group.

At the next meeting they explained the purpose and method of this technique and the group planned to use it. The members discussed what would be necessary to qualify an incident for study. They related their discussion to goals which they felt should be achieved. For what purpose or purposes would an analysis and study of the incident be made? What were reasonable expectations of its value for self-understanding and group functioning?

The analysis of the incidents provided useful insights into their group functioning. In varying degrees each person directly experienced himself as he participated in the group. Members found the method particularly useful in discussing matters on which there were conflicting ideas.

PROBLEM-DISCUSSION-ACTION METHOD

This is another form of action research which has proved useful. The group recognizes a problem, discusses it, develops a plan, acts upon it and evaluates it.

Eighteen persons (who comprised the total membership of a group) concluded that they would become acquainted more quickly and develop meaningful relationships if they spent part of the time in three small groups. They planned to discuss their progress after a few meetings. As a result of this planning, they spent part of the evening in small homogeneous groups and the remainder as a total group.

After three meetings they had serious doubts about their plan. They found that their attitudes and ideas were too much alike. Their discussions lacked challenge and the creative inputs of those with different perspectives. The members liked the idea of small groups but decided to make them heterogeneous.

They planned to include members with different points of view as a means of improving their interest and functioning. They also decided to use the results of an attitude inventory for the purpose of reformulating the groups. After they examined several inventories they chose the Dogmatism Scale (Form E)[8]. They remained anonymous, each one using a self-chosen number, and were placed in groups with as much variance in scores as possible. Their discussion of the results of using this kind of action research indicated great improvement and general satisfaction with the functioning of their small groups.

CONTENT ANALYSIS

Another method of action research which has proved itself quite useful is that of content analysis. The nature of the method is supplied in the title; it is an analysis of content. The content may be tape recordings, video tape recordings, or self-reports written anonymously by the members. These are analyzed by the members and leader, and the insights gained are incorporated into future meetings.

The leader and members plan the goals of such an undertaking, the kind of records to keep, ways of improving their validity (such as an immediate on-the-spot recording and no names required on any reports), criteria and methods of analysis. By planning cooperatively the research takes on meaning, involvement greatly increases and more learning results.

One group expressed an interest in trying to determine the degree of change in their personal attitudes and feelings from meeting to meeting. They decided to use self-reports. These were written under a self-chosen number at the close of each session. This was done by suggesting that each member choose a number and write the same number on each report. Each member described his feelings in relation to the interaction in the session. The leader also wrote a self-report. The members' self-reports were studied by the leader. He found these useful in helping him to gain insight into the dynamics of the process and of the goals and difficulties of each member. He compared his perceptions of his attitudes and functioning with those of the members.

After several sessions the counselor returned the self-reports. Each member analyzed his own and drew conclusions, planned goals and concentrated on them during the remaining sessions. They discussed these after five sessions and again at the end of ten sessions. They felt this was an interesting and useful method of self-study.

Evaluation Techniques

Each leader and the members develop and use methods of study and evaluation intrinsic in the situation. Different groups developed one or more of the following techniques (samples of which are provided at the end of this chapter, numbered as they are here): (1) A card for use by the observer; (2) and (3) member's self-evaluation scales; (4) a leader-evaluation scale; (5) a guide to the study and evaluation of self-reports; (6) one's development as a group member; (7) psychological needs in the group experience; (8) a means of analyzing the current stage in group process.

CARD FOR USE BY THE OBSERVER

One group planned the following: At the conclusion of the discussion the observer in the group passed a 4- by 6-inch card to each member. He asked each to respond to questions regarding his perception of the process and what improvement he planned to help the group and himself. The anonymously completed responses were passed to the observer, who relayed the information to the group.

MEMBER'S SELF-EVALUATION SCALES

Two other groups each planned to do a self-study using a rating scale. The members of each group cooperatively planned its own scale. In each case one small group developed the descriptive items. Since these mirror what the groups thought important they differ in what was considered important to evaluate.

In each case the scale was completed by each member at the end of the session under a self-chosen number. The observer or another member in each instance collated the results on the scale and informed the group of areas in which it was perceived that they were making progress and of those areas in which more attention was needed. The collation of the results was given to the leader who used it to gain insight regarding the members' self-perceptions of their progress.

LEADER-EVALUATION SCALE

The trainees or leaders of the small groups devised a scale to use in studying themselves and other leaders-in-training. This scale was completed anonymously by each member at the end of each session. They were then given to the leader of the session for review. He made a report to the group based on these and observations of his own functioning.

EVALUATING SELF-RENEWAL

Members generally choose the self-report as the means of understanding their attitudes, feelings and performance in each session. Each writes a running record of his feelings in relation to the interaction which took place and of his perceptions of the group process. These self-reports are completed at the end of each session under a self-chosen number. They are returned under their code number for analysis and summary as often as requested, generally at every fifth meeting.

These reports prove instructive to the leader. They help him to perceive the interaction and process development from the members' framework. Members also report it to be quite helpful in understanding their own feelings, their participation in the group and in setting goals.

DEVELOPMENT-AS-A-GROUP-MEMBER SCALE

After the members recognize the nature of group process and the importance of the attitudes and performance of the individual each becomes interested in some means of following his own development. One group planned a brief checklist and presented it to the whole group for comment. Following some changes they accepted the one given at the end of this chapter. Under a self-chosen number each member completed the form at the conclusion of every third or fourth meeting. These were given to the leader who studied them and returned them after each completion. The checklists served as a means for the leader and member to have a way of knowing in what areas and to what degree each was becoming a mature member of the group.

PSYCHOLOGICAL-NEEDS-IN-THE-GROUP-EXPERIENCE SCALE

One group discussed the individual needs which each brought to the group experience. They realized the dynamic way in which their need structure affected what they did. They recognized the need for balance in being helped to satisfy their needs and their willingness and responsibility to help one another satisfy his or her needs. They perceived some progression in the establishment of this balance as their experience in the group increased. As a means of clarifying, recognizing and understanding their progress they planned the inventory given at the end of this chapter. This inventory afforded them an opportunity for each to compare his perception of himself with those of other members and also with the goal he would like to attain. The members felt that the inventory helped them to become aware of their psychological behaviors in the group, and to study their progress in becoming interdependent. Some members completed one inventory each time, some every other time. Some discussed theirs with others. Those who did found this a means of exploring in depth their feelings about themselves and others.

GROUP PROCESS STAGES

Inventory results were used as a means of analyzing the current stage in group process. They were also used in discussions of involvement in group process in general and of members' own current involvement and working through of their problems.

The members' thinking led to a consideration of the steps or degree of progress experienced. They planned to read what had been written on the progressive steps in group process. The leader made several outlines available. After examination of these it was decided to use the one provided at the end of the chapter. On this form each member checked the stage of progress for himself and for the group and wrote explanations for his choices.

This form was referred to frequently by the group. The members found a great variance in their individual perceptions of the group stages. This led to some discussion and greater understanding of one another. They found much less difference in their perception of the stage in which the group was generally speaking. This led to discussion of what the group conceivably would be like as the members progressed to more mature group behavior.

SUMMARY

The leader will use the results of informal research to understand group process more fully and to improve the ongoing functioning of the group. This is especially necessary in helping those training to become leaders. The research undertaken or techniques developed should be planned with the trainees. This improves the possibility that the results will possess acceptable validity and will also have a wide range of influence. By sharing in the planning members become informed, cooperative and involved. Participants in a study should know in advance the possible ways in which the results could benefit them individually and as a group. The leader of the group should plan with the members to study his own practices to provide bases for understanding both his theoretical approach and the usefulness of his methods.

The leader must recognize that he is very likely to place too much confidence in research and techniques of studying the group. He will try to keep conclusions tentative and will be ready to accept new findings. He will replicate some of the studies and use of techniques for study, especially those in the areas which he perceives as most necessary and in which results would be most useful. He should avoid the easy tendency to make direct application of outside research to his own efforts. He should remain aware of the fact that conditions are likely to be so dissimilar as to make transfer of methods and conclusions unwise.

Needed Research

NECESSARY CONSIDERATIONS

Each leader should give thought to what he will do about research. Will he undertake it, and if so will it be informal or formal, or both? He must examine what to do in terms of his own functioning and the functioning of his various groups. He should recognize the need for research concerned with the general problems that confront all group leaders. Some of these research problems are suggested below.

1. What understandings need to be heightened, what skills need to be trained, what attitudes in interpersonal relationships need to be developed in order to help normally performing people to function more adequately in homes, schools, churches, businesses and organizations?

2. What are the optimal characteristics and training needed by those who engage in training others to be group leaders?

3. What should be significant differences in theory and method between those who lead groups of leaders-in-training and those who lead groups for persons interested in behavioral change?

4. What criteria can be used to guide enrollees in choosing between contrasting group experiences in both theory and method? It is not now known with any degree of certainty why some persons are helped by one method and not by another. It is a logical conclusion that no method will be suitable for everyone. Research could hopefully establish tentative criteria for choice.

5. Since the value of group process is in large measure dependent upon one's ability to listen, studies should be conducted to explore what is involved in the kind of listening necessary in group process. Further studies should elucidate the problems experienced in trying to become this kind of listener.

6. Both the group leader and the members should develop the ability to summarize ideas presented in the discussion. Since the vast majority experience great difficulty in doing this, research should be directed toward ascertaining possible reasons why this difficulty is of such magnitude. Such research should first explore the nature of the current attempts and then clarify the problems experienced. From this kind of research could emerge suggestions for improvement which in turn could be studied to determine their usefulness.

WITH INNER-CITY GROUPS

Special attention needs to be given to the study and research of inner-city groups. Because of the experiences and characteristics of the culturally deprived, inner-city children, youth and adults, research should be developed which is relevant to their special needs. If results are to be useful, practical hypotheses must arise from the experiences of group leaders who work with inner-city groups. Broadly described such research could clarify the perceptions of this group and the possible reasons for their particular reactions to emotionally laden situations.

Research goals are best oriented toward securing information which could be expected to help group leaders, counselors, teachers and others to work intelligently toward certain goals. These goals are improvement in impulse control; development of memory image (i.e., of their imagination abilities); reduction of need for aggression; and ability to perceive and examine alternatives.

These are very difficult research goals and the design presents a challenge to methodologists. Group leaders will need to use their ingenuity in planning and using various informal research means to test hypotheses related to any one of these goals.

CONCLUSIONS

The value of research and the use of techniques for studying the group are related directly to their relevance to problems for which more information and understanding are needed. Moreover findings must be expressed in terms which make them useful and capable of being applied.

FORM 1 Card for Use by the Observer (4″ by 6″ card)

Side 1
1. What was done which helped the group process?
2. What was the least helpful to the group process?

Side 2
1. What did you do to assist in the process?
2. What do you plan to do to improve in the next session?

FORM 2 Member's Self-Evaluation Scale

Date____________ Number____________

Circle the number in each category which agrees most with your conclusion regarding yourself.

1. LISTENING

I only partially hear the idea and not the person and what it means to him.				I hear the idea and to some degree understand the person and what the idea means to him.		
1	2	3	4	5	6	7

2. SENSE OF BELONGING

I feel strange and uneasy.				I feel comfortable and at ease.		
1	2	3	4	5	6	7

3. ACCEPTANCE OF OTHERS

I do not feel friendly toward some members or interested in them.				I feel kindly disposed toward and interested in the other members.		
1	2	3	4	5	6	7

continued on next page

4. CONCENTRATION

I have difficulty in following the strands of thought. — I follow the strands of thought with only slight difficulty.

1 2 3 4 5 6 7

5. PARTICIPATION

I participate nonverbally only — I participate nonverbally and often verbally

1 2 3 4 5 6 7

6. SILENCE

I am uncomfortable and do not think well. — I am able to use a silence to think on the subject.

1 2 3 4 5 6 7

7. CREATIVE DIFFERENCES

Differences of ideas make me uneasy — Differences of ideas are interesting to me

1 2 3 4 5 6 7

8. SENSE OF RESPONSIBILITY

I feel little responsibility for the discussion or in helping others — I feel responsible in relation to content, process, and member welfare

1 2 3 4 5 6 7

FORM 3 Member's Self-Evaluation Scale

Date____________ Number____________

Check the number on the rating scale that corresponds to your evaluation of yourself in each of the following categories. For example, if you feel that your responsible participation was lacking, check 1; if you feel that it was present, check 7; if you feel it was somewhere in between, check an appropriate number on the scale.

A. RESPONSIBLE PARTICIPATION I served my own needs. I watched from outside the group. I was "grinding my own ax."	1 2 3 4 5 6 7	A. RESPONSIBLE PARTICIPATION I was sensitive to the needs of our group.
B. LEADERSHIP I did not cooperate. I felt little responsibility.	1 2 3 4 5 6 7	B. LEADERSHIP I cooperated and was responsible to myself and the group.
C. COMMUNICATION OF IDEAS I did not listen. I did not understand. Ideas were ignored.	1 2 3 4 5 6 7	C. COMMUNICATION OF IDEAS I listened, and understood one another's ideas.
D. COMMUNICATION OF FEELINGS I did not listen and did not understand feelings.	1 2 3 4 5 6 7	D. COMMUNICATION OF FEELINGS I listened and understood, and recognized feelings.

continued on next page

E. AUTHENTICITY I was wearing a mask. I was being phony and acting a part. I was hiding my real self.	1 2 3 4 5 6 7	E. AUTHENTICITY I was revealing my honest self. I was engaged in authentic self-revelation.
F. ACCEPTANCE OF PERSONS I criticized, rejected, or ignored.	1 2 3 4 5 6 7	F. ACCEPTANCE OF PERSONS was an active part of my give-and-take. I recognized and respected the uniqueness of each person.
G. FREEDOM OF PERSONS I did not feel free to express my individuality.	1 2 3 4 5 6 7	G. FREEDOM OF PERSONS I felt free to express my individuality. I respected others as persons.
H. CLIMATE OF RELATIONSHIP I did not feel comfortable. I was uneasy and felt threatened.	1 2 3 4 5 6 7	H. CLIMATE OF RELATIONSHIP I felt mutual trust in which evidence of love for one another was apparent. The atmosphere was friendly and relaxed.
I. PRODUCTIVITY I was just coasting along.	1 2 3 4 5 6 7	I. PRODUCTIVITY I was digging hard and earnestly at work on a task. I created and achieved something.

FORM 4 Leader-Evaluation Scale

Date________________ Number________________

Circle the number in each category which agrees most with your conclusion regarding leader performance.

1. THE LEADER IS RESPONSIBLE.

Shows little responsibility for the discussion or in helping the members.				Is responsible in relation to content, process and member welfare.		
1	2	3	4	5	6	7

2. THE LEADER PROVIDES RESOURCES.

The leader provides little information or personal sharing.				The leader provides helpful information as needed and shares his feeling concerning it.		
1	2	3	4	5	6	7

3. THE LEADER PROVIDES STRATEGIES.

Does not provide as needed clarifying, summarizing and other functions.				Provides the necessary processes as needed for optimum functioning.		
1	2	3	4	5	6	7

continued on next page

4. THE LEADER COMMUNICATES.

Each member is more an object. The leader does not share his ideas.	Considers each member a person and is honest, open and real.

1 2 3 4 5 6 7

5. THE LEADER LISTENS.

Hears the idea but not the person and what it means to him.	Hears the idea and tries to understand the person and what the idea means to him.

1 2 3 4 5 6 7

6. THE LEADER TRUSTS.

He tries to assure outcomes; has a low level of expectancy; does not extend freedom.	He has a high level of expectancy; is permissive, and extends freedom in relation to acceptance of responsibility.

1 2 3 4 5 6 7

7. THE LEADER ENCOURAGES AND CONDUCTS EVALUATION.

Provides no encouragement or opportunity for evaluation.	The leader provides opportunity, initiates, encourages and assists members in evaluation.

1 2 3 4 5 6 7

FORM 5 Guide to Study and Evaluation of Self-Reports

Date________________ Number________________

Many students have found the following guide useful in studying their self-reports in order to understand their progress over the weeks of the course. The headings used are not arranged to indicate an order in which change may have taken place or to suggest that all these changes may have taken place. Other changes may have occurred and for these it may be useful to supply your own headings.

If after you have read your self-reports these headings appear to have some usefulness, try to indicate the degree using a five-point rating scale, 5 indicating the greatest degree, 1 the least. Also briefly describe or quote from the self-reports to support your rating.

1. A movement from self-centeredness to care for others.
   Rating
   Supportive Description or Quotes

2. A movement from doubt about self to trust of self.
   Rating
   Supportive Description or Quotes

3. A movement from secrecy to sharing.
   Rating
   Supportive Description or Quotes

continued on next page

4. A movement from unfreedom to freedom.
   Rating
   Supportive Description or Quotes

5. A movement from irresponsibility to a sense of responsibility.
   Rating
   Supportive Description or Quotes

6. A movement from mistrust to trust.
   Rating
   Supportive Description or Quotes

7. A movement from the need to receive help to a concern to give help.
   Rating
   Supportive Description or Quotes

FORM 6 Development-as-a-Group-Member Scale

Date________________ Number________________

1. FEELING OF BELONGINGNESS

I felt alone, uninvolved, unnecessary.

I felt that some members accepted me and that I was necessary.

I felt that most members were accepting me and that I was necessary.

I felt that everyone accepted me, that I was a necessary part of the group.

I felt full acceptance by everyone; that I was needed and that my contribution to the group was needed.

2. ACCEPTANCE OF RESPONSIBILITY OF MEMBERSHIP

I didn't feel any responsibility for anyone or the group as a whole.

I felt a little responsibility for contributing information but not for helping anyone to feel adequate.

I felt a little responsibility for helping one or two members to feel adequate and for contributing information.

I felt responsibility for contributing information, analyzing and presenting my analysis and evaluation of ideas presented and as well for helping several members to feel adequate and do likewise.

I felt responsibility for helping all the members and leader to feel adequate and to present information and their responses and as well felt a responsibility for myself to remain aware, accepting, to present ideas and conclusions concerning ideas presented by others.

3. LISTENING

I listen occasionally to another member and think about the ideas he presents.

I listen much of the time and often consider his ideas and sometimes what they may mean to him.

I listen most of the time and generally think about his ideas and what they mean to him.

As a general practice I listen to what everyone says, think about his ideas, how he feels about them and react to them verbally or nonverbally.

4. PARTICIPATION

I participated by listening most of the time.

I participated by listening and responding nonverbally (expression or nodding of head) some of the time.

I participated by listening and responding nonverbally much of the time and verbally occasionally.

I participated by listening and responding nonverbally most of the time and verbally frequently.

FORM 7 Psychological-Needs-in-the-Group-Experience Scale

Date________________ Number________________

This is a means for the analysis of your needs as they relate to the group process. Answer each statement in relation to (**a**) as you feel about it; (**b**) as most of the members of the group feel about it; (**c**) as you think you should feel about it. Use (1)—to indicate "almost none," (2)—"a little," (3)—"some," (4)—"much," and (5)—"very much."

1. I satisfy my personal needs in this experience.
   A________________ B ________________ C________________

2. I try not to use the experience to satisfy my personal needs.
   A________________ B ________________ C________________

3. I try to help others satisfy their needs rather than satisfy my own.
   A________________ B ________________ C________________

4. I feel I should satisfy my own needs as much as helping others to satisfy theirs.
   A________________ B ________________ C________________

5. I feel the intensity of my needs has been reduced because of the group experience.
   A________________ B ________________ C________________

6. I have more awareness of my needs because of the group experience.
   A________________ B ________________ C________________

7. I feel the other members of the group have needs similar to mine.
   A________________ B ________________ C________________

8. I feel I am becoming more aware of the needs of other members.

   A__________ B __________ C __________

9. I feel I am becoming more interested in the needs of other members.

   A__________ B __________ C __________

10. I feel less compulsion to satisfy my needs in the group.

    A__________ B __________ C __________

FORM 8 Group Process Stages

Date_______________ Number_______________

	Personal	Group
1. Establishment		
2. Check one another		
3. Check the leader		
4. Give rights to others		
5. Socialization		
6. What are we doing		
7. Can we trust one another, what shall we try to accomplish		
8. Experimentation try out, commitment to one another		
9. Responsibility for one another		
10. Creative relationship		

AUTHOR'S NOTES

1. Group Issues and Possibilities Today

1. With the publication of Darwin's *On the Origin of the Species* in 1859, the central hypotheses of evolution became more than the undocumented guessing of the eighteenth-century philosophers. It led to the acceptance of such concepts as: (1) geometric multiplication of offspring, (2) variation in structure and capability, (3) competition for the means of existence, and (4) the survival of the fittest.

2. John Dewey, *Liberalism and Social Action* (New York: G. P. Putnam's Sons, 1935), p. 51.

"One half of his [Dewey's] philosophy is devoted to an emphasis upon what in Christian theology is called the creatureliness of man, his involvement in biological and social process. The other half seeks a secure place for disinterested intelligence above the flux of process; and finds it in 'organized cooperative inquiry.'" From Reinhold Niebuhr, *The Nature and Destiny of Man*, Vol. I (New York: Charles Scribner's Sons, 1946), p. 111.

3. Charles Sanders Peirce, "How to Make Our Ideas Clear," *Popular Science Monthly*, January, 1878.

4. William James, "What Pragmatism Means," *Pragmatism and American Culture* (Boston: D. C. Heath Company, 1950), pp. 10-23.

5. Louis P. Thorpe, *Personality and Life* (New York: David McKay, 1949), p. 24.

6. *Ibid.*, p. 217. Thorpe has a clearly written description and evaluation of "crude" and "refined" pragmatism.

7. Robert Lynd and Helen M. Lynd, *Middletown in Transition* (New York: Harcourt, Brace and Co., 1937), p. 407. The Lynds list a number of aphorisms of American culture patterns

common in 1925-1935. For example: "Honesty is the best policy. But: Business is business, and a businessman would be a fool if he didn't cover his hand."

8. J. R. P. French, A. Kornhauser and A. Morrow (eds.), "Conflict and Cooperation in Industry," *The Journal of Social Issues* (1946), pp. 44-45.

9. *Cf.* Rollo May, *Man's Search for Himself* (New York: W. W. Norton and Co., 1953). An excellent companion book to Riesman's *The Lonely Crowd.*

10. For a full understanding of self-theory see Carl R. Rogers, *Client-Centered Therapy* (Boston: Houghton Mifflin Co., 1950). For a concise statement of the principles of self-theory, see C. Gratton Kemp, *Perspectives on the Group Process* (Boston: Houghton Mifflin Co., 1964).

11. Kurt Lewin describes his principles of behavioral change in an article with Paul Grabbe, "Conduct, Knowledge, and Acceptance of New Values," *The Journal of Social Issues*, 1 (1945), 56-64.

12. Hobart Mowrer describes his theory fully in *The New Group Therapy* (Princeton: D. Van Nostrand Co., 1964). See p. 8 for the point mentioned here.

13. Helen Durkin elaborates on this point concerning the therapeutic value of ventilation in *The Group in Depth* (New York: International Universities Press, 1964), p. 60.

14. Samuel Beck, "Emotional Experience as a Necessary Constituent in Knowing" in Martin L. Reymert (ed.), *Feelings and Emotions* (New York: McGraw-Hill Book Co., 1950), pp. 59-108 (an interesting and unusual chapter).

15. The new understandings regarding the function of emotion are described by R. W. Leeper, "A Motivational Theory of Emotion to Replace Emotion as Disorganized Response," *Psychological Review*, 55 (1948), 5-21.

16. Erich Fromm, *Escape from Freedom* (New York: Holt, Rinehart and Winston, 1941), p. 19. An excellent source explaining how we lose our personhood.

17. J. McV. Hunt, "Intrinsic Motivation and Its Role in Psychological Development," in *Nebraska Symposium on Motivation, 1965* (Lincoln: University of Nebraska Press, 1965).

18. Harmon Smith has a provocative analysis of pseudo-love appearances in "When Love Becomes Excarnate," in John Bennett *et al., Storm over Ethics* (St. Louis: Bethany Press, 1967).

19. For an understanding of the meaning of "A Personal Center," see C. Gratton Kemp, "From Person to Person," chap. 13 in *Intangibles in Counseling* (Boston: Houghton Mifflin, 1967).

20. L. Thomas Hopkins, *The Emerging Self in School and Home* (New York: Harper & Bros., 1954), p. 195. This is an excellent discussion of the organic group and the need-experience process.

21. Hubert S. Coffey, "Socio and Psyche Group Process: Integrative Concepts," quoted in *Perspectives on the Group Process*, by C. Gratton Kemp (Boston: Houghton Mifflin Co., 1970 ed.), p. 48.

2. *The Nature of the Small Group*

1. D. Krech and R. S. Crutchfield, *Theory and Problems of Social Psychology* (New York: McGraw-Hill Book Co., 1948), p. 18.

2. R. B. Cattell, "New Concepts for Measuring Leadership in Terms of Group Syntality," *Human Relations*, 4 (1951), 161-184.

3. *Group Patterns*

1. L. Thomas Hopkins in *The Emerging Self in School and Home, op. cit.*, has helpful explanations of the aggregate or authoritarian group.

2. C. Gratton Kemp in *Perspectives on the Group Process, op. cit.*, has useful explanations of the foundations and nature of the democratic group.

3. Thomas Gordon, *Group-Centered Leadership* (Boston:

Houghton Mifflin Co., 1955). This is one of the best sources for a comprehensive description of the group-centered group.

4. A comprehensive and authentic treatment of the T group is given in Leland P. Bradford *et al.*, *T Group Theory and Laboratory Method* (New York: John Wiley and Sons, 1964).

5. Arthur Burton (ed.), *Encounter: The Theory and Practice of Encounter Groups* (San Francisco: Jossey-Bass, 1969), p. 13.

6. Based on Carl R. Rogers, "The Process of the Basic Encounter Group," in J. F. T. Bugental, *The Challenge of Humanistic Psychology* (New York: McGraw-Hill Book Co., 1967).

7. The chief source is Paul Bergevin and John McKinley, *Participation Training in Adult Education* (St. Louis: Bethany Press, 1965).

4. Group Process

1. A full-length discussion of group process is presented in chap. 4 of *Foundations of Group Counseling*, by C. Gratton Kemp (New York: McGraw-Hill Book Co., 1970).

2. This most important skill of listening is treated by Thomas Gordon in *Group-Centered Leadership*, and by C. Gratton Kemp in *Perspectives on the Group Process*. Learning to listen from the speaker's point of view is discussed by Carl R. Rogers in *Client-Centered Therapy, op. cit.*, and in *Becoming a Person* (Boston: Houghton Mifflin, 1961).

3. Helpful information on observation and the observer is provided by Kenneth Benne and Paul Sheats in "Functional Roles of Group Members," *The Journal of Social Issues*, 4 (1948), 42-47.

4. A good explanation of the "linking function" is given by Thomas Gordon in *Group-Centered Leadership, op. cit.*

5. There is an excellent analysis of the problems involved in summarization in D. E. Broadbent's "Flow of Information within the Organism," *Journal of Verbal Learning and Verbal Behavior*, 2 (1963), 34-39.

5. *The Leader*

1. Jack R. Gibb, "Fear and Façade: Defensive Management," in *Science and Human Affairs,* Richard E. Farson (ed.), (Palo Alto: Science and Behavior Books, 1965), pp. 197-214. This is an excellent discussion of two contrasting views in management due to differences in leader qualities.

2. Murray Ross and Charles E. Hendry, *New Understandings of Leadership* (New York: Association Press, 1957), pp. 43-44. The chapter on the qualities of the leader is useful and clearly written.

3. Carl Jung, *Psychological Types* (New York: Harcourt, Brace, 1923), p. 577.

4. Paul Tillich, *The Courage to Be* (New Haven: Yale University Press, 1952), p. 110.

5. A concisely written article by C. Gratton Kemp presents distinctions in leadership functioning in *Perspectives on the Group Process, op. cit.* See Part Four, Section C, "Leadership Functioning."

6. The ethical viewpoint of leader functioning is interestingly presented by Theodore Brameld in "Ethics of Leadership," *Adult Leadership,* Vol. 4 (June, 1955).

7. Background material helpful in understanding the various types of leadership is given in Section B, "Theories of Leadership," by C. Gratton Kemp *et al., Perspectives on the Group Process, op. cit.*

8. Bradford *et al., T Group Theory and Laboratory Method* and *Process of the Basic Encounter Group,* both mentioned previously, are useful in understanding particular kinds of leadership functioning.

9. There are many indications that the focus of members' concerns has changed. Formerly they may have asked, "What is man? How does he perform?" Now many are asking, "Who is man? Who am I?" If this is so, leaders need to be able to hear the existential concerns of members. Leroy F. Troutner discusses

this change in focus and its implications for leaders in "Confrontation between Experimentalism and Existentialism: From Dewey to Heidegger and Beyond," *Harvard Educational Review*, 39 (1969), 124-154.

6. *The Group Member*

1. A further discussion of what members contribute to the group may be found in Hopkins, *The Emerging Self in School and Home, op. cit.*, pp. 216-220.

2. An unusual perspective is presented by Morton Alpren in his article, "How Do Groups Test the Leader's Willingness to Share Decisions?" in *The Educational Forum*, 19 (1955), 467-470.

3. Kenneth D. Benne and Paul Sheats, "Functional Roles of Group Members," *The Journal of Social Issues*, 4 (1949), 42-47.

4. Group members function in terms of their perceptions of themselves and others. The function of perception is interestingly described by Arthur W. Combs and Donald Snygg, *Individual Behavior* (New York: Harper & Row, 1959), pp. 150-156.

5. Milton Rokeach, *The Open and Closed Mind* (New York: Basic Books, 1960), p. 66. Qualities needed for persons to become adequate and helpful group members are discussed by Carl R. Rogers in his book, *On Becoming a Person, op. cit.*, pp. 338-346.

6. C. Gratton Kemp, "Self Perception in Relation to Open and Closed Belief Systems," *Journal of General Psychology*, 70 (1964), 341-344.

7. C. Gratton Kemp, *Foundations of Group Counseling* (New York: McGraw-Hill, 1970), p. 248.

7. *Special Problems in Interaction*

1. One concept of group size is described by Herbert Thelen in "Group Dynamics in Instruction: The Principle of Least Group Size," *School Review*, 57 (1949), 139-148.

James A. Schellenberg studied group size in relation to academic achievement. He describes the study and presents his findings in his article, "Group Size as a Factor in Success of Academic Discussion Groups," *Journal of Educational Sociology,* 33 (1959), 73-79.

A. P. Hare, "A Study of Interaction and Consensus in Different Sized Groups," *American Sociological Review,* 17 (1952), 261-267.

R. C. Ziller, "Group Size: A Determinant of the Quality and Stability of Group Decisions," *Sociometry,* 20 (1957), 165-173.

Psathas found in his review of the literature that with increase in size of the group, members experience less direct involvement. See G. Psathas, "Overview of Process Studies in Group Psychotherapy," *International Journal of Group Psychotherapy,* 17 (1967), 225-235.

2. D. Patrick Hughes takes a positive view of silence in his article, "The Silent Period in Group Process," *The Clearing House,* 32 (1957), 230-231.

3. Resistance is generally considered an important dynamic in involvement in group process. Hazel Osborn writes clearly on this topic in her article, "Some Factors of Resistance Which Affect Group Participation," *The Group,* 2 (1949), 9-11.

Merle Ohlsen has a helpful chapter on resistance in his book, *Group Counseling* (New York: Holt, Rinehart and Winston, 1970), chap. 6.

4. A further statement on the functioning of the will can be read in C. Gratton Kemp's book, *Intangibles in Counseling, op. cit.* See chap. 4, "The Will."

A classic reading on involvement with reference to the will is Rollo May's *Love and Will* (New York: W. W. Norton Co., 1969).

5. There is an excellent discussion of conflict in the article by Harry and Bonaro Overstreet, "Creative Handling of Conflict," *The Saturday Review,* February 20, 1954.

6. Further points of view on group functioning are expressed by Thomas Hopkins in his book, *The Emerging Self in School and Home, op. cit.,* pp. 216-220.

8. Putting Group Process to Work

1. The proper use of group process in conferences varies to some degree with each situation. To use group process uncritically is unlikely to gain the results desired, and such procedure conceals its possibilities and best use. Group-process usage should never subordinate people to plans. However, group process demands more planning than we usually give when we use it and sometimes more productive imagination than we are in the habit of using.

2. Leland Bradford has keen insight into the possibilities of using group process in teaching. He expresses his views in two articles in an interesting and helpful manner: "Developing Potentialities through Class Groups," *Teachers College Record,* 61 (1960), pp. 443-450; and "Group Forces Affecting Learning," *Journal of the National Association of Women Deans and Counselors,* 33 (1960), 116-120.

A candid description of difficulties which a teacher meets in using group process and the creative handling of conflicts is delightfully depicted by Agnes L. Kemp in "We Developed Togetherness," *Children's Religion,* October, 1955, pp. 13-15.

3. Fritz Redl and David Wineman, *The Aggressive Child* (New York: The Free Press, 1957), p. 258.

4. Carl Jung, *Psychological Types* (New York: Harcourt, Brace, 1923), p. 577.

5. Paul Tillich differentiates between "courage to be as a part" and "courage to be," in his book *The Courage to Be* (New Haven: Yale University Press, 1952), chaps. 4 and 5.

6. Milton Rokeach clarifies and describes the "party-line" thinker in *The Open and Closed Mind, op. cit.,* pp. 225-242.

7. C. Gratton Kemp in his research with freshman college students entitled "Improvement of Critical Thinking in Relation to Open-Closed Belief Systems" (*Journal of Experimental Education,* 1963, Vol. 31, pp. 321-323) found five factors which decreased efficiency: (*a*) ignoring, distorting or omitting some of

the given data; (*b*) including additional words or ideas; (*c*) a rigid, often nonadaptive approach; (*d*) failure to synthesize or a poor quality of synthesis; (*e*) failure to evaluate conclusions or incompleteness of evaluation.

8. The results of using this method of change in industry are described in Schuyler D. Hoslett, *Human Factors in Management* (New York: Harper & Bros., 1951), chap. 4.

9. Jack R. Gibb compares "defensive" and "participative" management in "Fear and Façade: Defensive Management," *op. cit.*

10. J. R. P. French, A. Kornhauser, and A. Morrow (eds.), "Conflict and Cooperation in Industry," *The Journal of Social Issues* (1946), pp. 44-45.

11. Kurt Lewin and Paul Grabbe, "Conduct, Knowledge, and Acceptance of New Values," *op. cit.*, pp. 45-64.

12. A description of research and the results using small groups in various kinds of industry is presented by Rensis Likert in his chapter, "An Emerging Theory of Organization, Leadership, and Management," in Luigi Petrullo and Bernard M. Bass (eds.), *Leadership and Interpersonal Behavior* (New York: Holt, Rinehart and Winston, 1961). The conclusion reached by five authorities engaged in research between 1953-1957 was that supervisors and managers who are aware of and use group process tend to achieve better results.

9. *Studying the Group*

1. M. S. Sheldon and A. C. Sorenson, "On the Use of the Q-technique in Educational Evaluation and Research," *Journal of Experimental Education*, 10 (1960), 143-151.

2. Carl R. Rogers, "The Therapeutic Relationship: Recent Theory and Research," *Australian Journal of Psychology*, 17 (1965), 95-108.

3. Donald T. Campbell and Julian C. Stanley, "Experimental Designs for Research in Teaching," in N. L. Gage (ed.) *Handbook of Research on Teaching* (Chicago: Rand McNally, 1963), chap. 5.

4. Stephen M. Corey, *Action Research to Improve School Practice* (New York: Bureau of Publications, Teachers College, Columbia University, 1953), p. 161.

5. Carter V. Good, *Essentials of Educational Research.* (New York: Appleton-Century-Crofts, 1966), p. 254.

6. John C. Flanagan, "The Critical Incident Technique," *Psychological Bulletin,* 51 (1954), 327-358.

7. Lewis B. Mayhew, "The Critical Incident Technique in Educational Evaluation," *Journal of Educational Research,* 49 (1956), 591-598.

8. Milton Rokeach, *The Open and Closed Mind* (New York: Basic Books, 1960), pp. 73ff.